Baby Names: Th
Or

By R

GW00792413

Speaking of....

Is your significant other, best friend, mother or child adamant about a name they want you to use? Has your sister-in-law stolen the name you'd been dreaming of? Is there a name you love, but it reminds you of someone you'd rather never think about again? My advice is to find that name in here and then find a happy alternative.

Where did I get all my names you ask? Well, I have to admit that I am something of a name nut. I've been keeping lists for years starting at about 12 years old. It's embarrassing but true. I also scoured the internet for every possible way to search for names. I did not copy and paste huge lists from sites. Every name was considered and selected and then categorized for this book. I also trolled mom forums, read articles about baby name trends, and listened for names in everyday life. I am looking forward to not thinking about names for a while.

Alas, I am not including all name meanings. I do apologize. I have highlighted a few names after each section with origin, meaning, and popularity rankings. If meanings are super important to you, remember that the meaning and/or origin can change with the spelling. Also remember that a name can be personally meaningful without the need to worry about what it meant in Old English. My husband and I named our son after a mountain near where we met.

There are a few other items to bear in mind. Check the names you like for infamous

The first thing you'll notice about this book is the way it is organized. My book is <u>not</u> alphabetical by first letter. This made it harder for me to put together, but I do believe it will be *much* easier for expecting parents to read through. The names in my book are alphabetized by their ending *sound*s. For example, the boy names Casey and Pacey are next to each other. There are over 3,000 names here, but my lists are not padded with alternate spellings of the same name, i.e.: Rachel and Rachael. If it doesn't affect pronunciation, I've only listed a name once. Some people like traditional spellings, some like names spelled phonetically, and some like to be original. I will leave that up to you.

By clustering names with the same ending, you'll get a better feel for a name you're considering. Look at Dana, Danna, Deanna, Deena, Dena, Diana, and Dinah. One letter change can make a big difference. You'll see the most common naming patterns we use, such as the use of -ah endings for girls and -er endings for boys. Do you like a traditional name, but would like a funky variation on it? It's easily done using this book.

Next on the agenda, are you really considering naming your child Gormilleah or Cluneah? In my book, not EVERY possible name is listed. If you want to slog through 10,000 names in alphabetical order, be my guest. This is also not a rehash of the same 100 names you'll find in any search. The best place is right in the middle. I've included a mix of traditional, modern, cultural and biblical options you won't be embarrassed to show your spouse.

connections. I don't recommend naming your little man Adolf, Manson, or Hannibal. And for girls, Drizella brings up images of the ugly step-sister in Cinderella. These days there are so many choices. Not everyone will love the name you choose, and that's okay. However, if no one seems to like it, consider why. Picture your child beyond infancy. How do they like their name in elementary school, in high school, and as an adult? After all, it is *their* name.

The popularity of a name can often be tied to a celebrity, or a character from a popular movie or book. Sometimes the correlation is dramatic. For example, Reese Witherspoon helped Reese turn from primarily a baby boy name to a popular name for baby girls. These trends may make some parents squeamish. However, this has been happening since the beginning of time, as people named their children after kings and queens or war heroes or Biblical prophets. I don't believe people are dying to name their kids after celebrities so much as a celebrity can normalize an uncommon name much faster than the rest of us. A strange name can suddenly sound familiar and everyone will know how to pronounce it and spell it. So don't worry if you like a name that (gasp!) belongs to a character from Twilight.

For reference, here are the top 10 baby names from around the world for 2015 (unless noted otherwise). I picked countries that have up to date records and have names Americans might like to borrow. The U.S. ranking is in parentheses next to the top 10 for other countries (if the name was in the U.S. top 1000). It's interesting to see how names spread.

Take for example, Amelia. This #1 pick in England and Wales is #9 in British Columbia and #2 in Ireland. Amelia reached top 100 in the U.S. in 2004 and was #12 in 2015. I predict U.S. top 10 next year.

Top 10 U.S. Baby Names

1. Noah	Emma
2. Liam	Olivia
3. Mason	Sophia
4. Jacob	Ava
5. William	Isabella
6. Ethan	Mia
7. James	Abigail
8. Alexander	Emily
9. Michael	Charlotte
10. Benjamin	Harper

Australia's Top 10 Baby Names (U.S. rank in parentheses)

1. Oliver (#19)	Olivia (#2)
2. William (#5)	Charlotte (#9)
3. Jack (#40)	Mia (#6)

4. Noah (#1)	Ava (#4)
5. Thomas (#51)	Amelia (#12)
6. Lucas (#16)	Emily (#8)
7. James (#7)	Sophie (#104)
8. Ethan (#6)	Chloe (#17)
9. Alexander (#8)	Ruby (#83)
10. Liam (#2)	Grace (#19)

British Columbia's Top 10 Baby Names (Provinces track their own vital statistics – rather than an overall count by Canada)

1. Oliver (#19)	Emma (#1)
2. Ethan (#6)	Olivia (#2)
3. Liam (#2)	Emily (#8)
4. Benjamin (#10)	Sophia (#3)
5. Lucas (#16)	Ava (#4)
6. Alexander (#8)	Chloe (#17)
7. Jacob (#4)	Charlotte (#9)
8. Mason (#3)	Abigail (#7)
9. William (#5)	Amelia (#12)
10. Hunter (#41)	Ella (#18)

England & Wales Top 10 Baby Names (2014 data)

1. Oliver (#19)	Amelia (#12)
2. Jack (#40)	Olivia (#2)
3. Harry (#781)	Isla (#141)
4. Jacob (#4)	Emily (#8)
5. Charlie (#229)	Poppy
6. Thomas (#51)	Ava (#4)
7. George (#136)	Isabella (#5)
8. Oscar (#181)	Jessica (#206)
9. James (#7)	Lily (#25)
10. William (#5)	Sophie (#104)

France's Top 10 Baby Names (2010)

1. Nathan (#38)	Emma (#1)
2. Lucas (#16)	Léa (#738)
3. Enzo (#330)	Chloé (#17)
4. Léo (#91)	Manon
5. Louis (#297)	Inés
6. Hugo (#432)	Lola (#224)
7. Gabriel (#22)	Jade (#126)

8. Éthan (#6)	Camille (#246)
9. Jules	Sarah (#58)
10. Mathis (#)	Louise

Germany's Top 10 Baby Names

1. Maximilian (#437)	Sophie (#104)
2. Alexander (#8)	Marie (#564)
3. Paul (#200)	Sophia (#3)
4. Elias (#100)	Maria (#109)
5. Luis (#106)	Emma (#1)
6. Luka (#522)	Mia (#6)
7. Ben (#740)	Hannah (#28)
8. Leon (#314)	Emilia (#592)
9. Lukas (#253)	Anna (#44)
10. Noah (#1)	Johanna (#541)

Ireland's Top 10 Baby Names (based on passport applications for children born in 2015)

1. Daniel (#12)	Emily (#8)
2. James (#7)	Amelia (#12)

3. Jack (#40)	Emma (#1)
4. Conor (#477)	Mia (#6)
5. Adam (#73)	Anna (#44)
6. Liam (#2)	Olivia (#2)
7. Noah (#1)	Hannah (#28)
8. Cillian	Sophie (#104)
9. Oliver (#19)	Aoife
10. Harry (#781)	Grace (#19)

Italy's Top 10 Baby Names (2014 data)

1. Francesco	Sofia (#14)
2. Alessandro (#680)	Giulia
3. Lorenzo (#216)	Aurora (#79)
4. Andrea	Giorgia
5. Leonardo (#103)	Martina (#922)
6. Mattia	Emma (#1)
7. Matteo (#191)	Greta (#573)
8. Gabriele	Chiara
9. Riccardo	Sara (#162)
10. Tommaso	Alice (#87)

Netherland's Top 10 Baby Names (2014)

1. Liam (#2)	Emma (#1)
2. Luuk	Sophie (#104)
3. Sem	Julia (#89)
4. Daan	Anna (#44)
5. Lucas (#16)	Mila (#53)
6. Milan (#424)	Tess
7. Noah (#1)	Fenna
8. Levi (#8)	Lotte
9. Bram	Eva (#75)
10. Jesse (#178)	Zoe (#33)

Norway's Top 10 Baby Names (2014 data)

1. Lucas (#16)	Nora (#41)
2. William (#5)	Emma (#1)
3. Markus (#865)	Sara (#162)
4. Emil	Sofie
5. Oskar	Emilie (#867)
6. Mathias (#561)	Anna (#44)
7. Magnus (#860)	Linnea

8. Filip	Thea (#)
9. Jakob (#523)	Maja
10. Aksel	Sofia (#14)

Portugal's Top 10 Baby Names (2014 data)

1. João	Maria (#109)
2. Rodrigo (#460)	Matilde
3. Francisco (#247)	Leonor
4. Martim	Beatriz
5. Santiago (#127)	Mariana (#296)
6. Tomás (#719)	Carolina (#430)
7. Afonso	Ana (#211)
8. Duarte	Inês
9. Miguel (#161)	Sofia (#14)
10. Guilherme	Margarida

Spain's Top 10 Baby Names (2014 data)

1. Hugo (#432)	Luciá (#225)
2. Daniel (#12)	Mariá (#109)
3. Pablo (#393)	Martina (#922)

4. Alejandro (#180)	Paula (#889)
5. Álvaro (#909)	Daniela (#200)
6. Adrián (#58)	Sofia (#14)
7. David (#18)	Valeria (#161)
8. Martin (#276)	Carla (#873)
9. Mario (#284)	Sara (#162)
10. Diego (#124)	Alba

Sweden's Top 10 Baby Names

1. William (#5)	Elsa (#487)
2. Lucas (#16)	Alice (#87)
3. Liam (#2)	Maja
4. Oscar (#181)	Saga
5. Elias (#100)	Ella (#18)
6. Hugo (#432)	Lilly (#139)
7. Oliver (#19)	Olivia (#2)
8. Charlie (#229)	Ebba
9. Axel (#123)	Wilma
10. Vincent (#109)	Julia (#89)

On to the alphabetical ending lists! Here are a few navigational hints: Vowel endings will be first, then consonant endings alphabetically. Remember, the names are organized by sound and not spelling. For example, half of the girl names ending in "ia" are pronounced "ee-a" as in Mia, and the other half are pronounced "sha" as in "Alicia." I apologize if some of the names can be pronounced more than one way. I tried to go with the most common pronunciation.

Where I've added information from the Social Security Administration http://www.ssa.gov/oact/babynames/ there will be two numbers I refer to. One is the ranking number for the top 1000 baby names of each year. For example, Noah was the #1 ranking baby name for boys in 2015. I may also refer to the number of babies given that name. For example, there were 19,511 baby boys given the name Noah in 2015. Unless otherwise stated, I'm referring to babies in the U.S.A. I will also add the # symbol to the front of a ranking number to help identify it. For privacy reasons, the social security administration will not list a name if less than 5 babies received it. It's quite possible no one received the name that year. I will just say, 'less than 5 babies received this name' or 'not listed for 2015.'

Girl names ending with an "ah" sound

Alba, Ebba, Reba, Sabra

Alba (Latin, meaning "white") is a top ten name in Spain, but there were only 157 baby girls named Alba in the U.S. in 2015. Ebba (strength) is a top 10 name in Sweden. 13 U.S. baby girls were named Ebba in 2015. 14 were named Reba. Reba, a form of Rebecca, means "to bind." I like Sabra, a Hebrew that means "to rest" or "patient." It is also the name of an Israeli prickly plant, and can refer to a native born Israeli. There were 8 U.S. baby girls named Sabra in 2015.

Alda, Alejandra, Alexandra, Alondra, Amanda, Andra, Andrea, Audra, Belinda, Binda, Brenda, Chandra, Cassandra, Celinda, Cressida, Deidre, Esmeralda, Giada, Gilda, Giselda, Glenda, Glinda, Golda, Hilda, Ida, Jacinda, Jada, Kendra, Kindra, Linda, Mathilda, Matilda, Melinda, Merida, Merinda, Miranda, Naida, Nerida, Orinda, Phaedra, Querida, Randa, Rhoda, Sandra, Sidda, Sidra, Sondra, Vada, Vida, Zaida

Have you considered Audra, meaning "noble strength"? There were 190 U.S. baby girls named Audra in 2015. Cressida is a Greek/Germanic name that means "Golden." This Shakespearean name is rarely used, with only 10 U.S. baby girls named Cressida in 2015. Merida is a Scottish Disney princess, but the name is Latin and a place name for a city in Spain (and Merida, Mexico). There were 99 baby girls named Merida in the U.S. in 2015.

Adelpha, Elfa, Jaffa, Josepha, Kalifa, Ketifa, Latifa, Letifa, Stepha, Zilpha

These names are so uncommonly used that they were not listed in 2015, with the exception of Latifa. There were 9 baby girls named Latifa, an Arabic name meaning "gentle" or "pleasant." I also like Jaffa. It's a Hebrew name that's easy to pronounce and means "beautiful."

Anga, Inga, Olga, Senga

Anga is a Swahili name that means "sky." Less than 5 baby girls in the U.S. were named this in 2015. Inga is an old fashioned name with many European origins and generally means "belonging to Ing," but also in some instances "Hero's daughter." Inga was in the top 1000 baby girl names from 1880 to 1914. Only 22 U.S. baby girls were given the name Inga in 2015.

Aja, Deja, Georgia

Is Georgia on your mind? Georgia is the feminine form of George – meaning "farmer." This name is on the move all over the world (top 100 in many European countries), but it definitely has an American appeal to it. Georgia was in the top 100 U.S. baby girl names for most of the 1800s, and has remained a steady favorite. Its lowest point was in 1986 at #725. Georgia was #230 in 2015.

America, Anca, Angelica, Anika, Becca, Bianca, Blanca, Corsica, Danica, Erica, Francesca, Jenica, Jessica, Kamika, Lenka, Mariska, Micah, Minka, Monica, Nika, Rebecca, Seneca, Tamika, Veronica, Vivica, Zelenka

Jessica was in the #1 or #2 spot from 1981-1997. Other –ca names like Monica, Erica, and Rebecca ranked in the top 100 during those years. Take a look at Mariska (Hungarian – "Of the sea"). This name was brought into the mainstream by the actress Mariska Hargitay. Only a handful of babies were given the name Mariska every year until a bump starting in 2004. Mariska's best year was 2007, with 107 U.S. baby girls. There were 30 baby girls named Mariska in 2015. I also like Bianca, a Shakespearean name and the Italian version of Blanche, meaning "fair" or "white." Bianca came into the top 1000 U.S. baby girl names in 1973 and was #379 in 2015.

Adela, Akeila, Angela, Antonella, Arabella, Ariella, Aviella, Bella, Briella, Calla, Camilla, Carla, Carmela, Charla, Consuela, Daniella, Darla, Delilah, Della, Donatella, Donella, Donla, Ella, Enola, Estrella, Fabiola, Finella, Finola, Fiorella, Gabriella, Gisela, Graciela, Ila, Isabella, Isela, Isla, Isola, Jamila, Jayla, Kailua, Kalila, Kayla, Kella, Kyla, Leila, Lila, Lola, Luella, Mahala, Marcella, Marla, Mella, Michaela, Mila, Mirabella, Nala, Neela, Nicola, Nola, Nyla, Orla, Pamela, Paula, Pella, Perla, Petronella, Priscilla, Rilla, Saylah, Selah, Shayla, Sheila, Shyla, Skyla, Stella, Sula, Sybella, Tula, Twyla, Tyla, Ursula, Viola, Willa, Zella, Zola

There are many Italian and Spanish names in this group, from Isabella to Carmela. Perla is getting a lot of attention these days. It is the Spanish variation of Pearl and reached the top 1000 U.S. baby girl names in 1979. Perla ranked #645 in 2015. Also take a closer look at Fiorella. Although not popular in the U.S., it is a beautiful Italian name meaning, "little flower." 47 baby girls in the U.S. were named Fiorella in 2015.

Alma, Carma, Cosima, Dalma, Delma, Desma, Dharma, Dima, Elma, Emma, Fatima, Gemma, Halima, Luma, Naima, Neema, Noma, Norma, Padma, Paloma, Salma, Selma, Talma, Thelma, Uma, Wilma

Emma skyrocketed to the top of the U.S. charts in 2008, but a new name to try out might be Cosima, pronounced KO-see-mah. This Greek name is derived from the word kosmos, meaning "order, harmony, beauty, universe." 20 baby girls received the name Cosima in the U.S. in 2015. Also look at Halima, pronounced ha-LEE-mah. Halima is an Arabic name meaning "gentle." 73 baby girls in the U.S. were named Halima in 2015.

Adina, Adriana, Alana, Alina, Angelina, Anna, Ariana, Arina, Athena, Audrina, Avalina, Aviana, Avonna, Bernina, Bettina, Brenna, Brianna, Brina, Brynna, Carmina, Carolena, Carolina, China, Cinna, Corina, Cortina, Christina, Dana, Danna, Deanna, Deena, Delanna, Delfina, Dena, Desdemona, Devonna, Diana, Dinah, Edna, Elena, Eliana, Enna, Eviana, Fenna, Fiona, Georgiana, Gianna, Gina, Gloriana, Guiliana, Halina, Hannah, Helena, Henna, Ileana, Ilona, Indiana, Ivanna, Jana, Jenna, Johanna, Juliana, Juna, Karina, Katarina, Katrina, Keilana, Kenna, Kohana, Lana, Leena, Lena, Leona, Liliana, Livana, Lorna, Lovina, Luna, Makenna, Mariana, Marina, Marlena, Melina, Milena, Mina, Mona, Montana, Nina, Nona, Patina, Paulina, Ramona, Ravenna, Regina, Reyna, Riana, Rhona, Roxana, Sabrina, Savannah, Sedona, Selena, Seraphina, Serena, Shaena, Shanna, Shauna, Sheena, Shona, Shoshanna, Senna, Sienna, Solana, Sophina, Susanna, Sylvana, Tana, Tatiana, Tiana, Tina, Toriana, Trina, Una, Valentina, Vanna, Verbena, Verna, Vienna, Viviana, Wenonah, Wilhelmina, Wynona, Ximena, Zhanna

There are many place names in this group, including Ravenna (an Italian city), Montana (state), Savannah (city), Makenna (Makena, Hawaii), Vienna (capital of Austria), Sedona (city), and Helena (city). I like Solana, a little used Spanish name meaning "sunshine." There were 65 U.S. baby girls named Solana in 2015. Solana could be a unique alternative to the increasingly popular Sienna (#229 in 2015). I believe Sienna will move into the top 100 baby names in the U.S. in the next few years. It's already top 100 in countries like Australia and Canada.

Pippa, Phillipa, Olympia, Opa, Zilpah

Kate Middleton's sister recently brought Pippa (a condensed version of Phillipa meaning "lover of horses") to the attention of baby namers. 92 U.S. baby girls were named Pippa in 2015. Also take a closer look at Opa. It means "owl" in Choctaw (Native American origin). Less than 5 U.S. baby girls were named Opa in 2015.

Akira, Allegra, Amara, Aura, Aurora, Barbara, Camira, Ciara, Clara, Cora, Cyra, Dara, Deborah, Devorah, Dora, Elanora, Elara, Elora, Endora, Eudora, Electra, Farah, Flora, Hera, Isidora, Jora, Kamora, Kara, Kefira, Keturah, Kierra, Kimora, Kira, Kumara, Lara, Laura, Leonora, Leora, Lyra, Lystra, Mara, Maura, Mira, Myra, Nera, Nevara, Nira, Nora, Oprah, Petra, Prospera, Samara, Samira, Sapphira, Sarah, Shakira, Shera, Shira, Sierra, Sonora, Tamara, Tara, Tierra, Tyra, Vera, Viera, Yadira, Zara, Zura

I personally love the –ra ending sound. There are many good choices here, both popular (Kira has been in the top 1000 since 1969 with a major jump to the top 200-300 in the 1990s) and the uncommon (Viera – meaning "truth," has never been in the top 1000). Disney's Sleeping Beauty came out in 1959, but didn't have much effect on the ranking for Aurora (Latin for "dawn"). Aurora stayed in the #700-#900 range in the decades following and grew increasingly popular starting in the 1990s. Aurora jumped into the top 100 in 2015 for the first time ever at #79.

Adessa, Alyssa, Brisa, Carissa, Chessa, Clarissa, Cressa, Eloisa, Elsa, Isa, Isla, Janessa, Janissa, Jessa, Julissa, Larissa, Lisa, Marissa, Marquesa, Melissa, Nessa, Nerissa, Odessa, Reesa, Rosa, Rossa, Talissa, Teresa, Tessa, Tressa, Vanessa

Have you considered Brisa? A Spanish name that means "breeze," only 192 U.S. baby girls were named this in 2015. Melissa held the #2 spot for three years in the 1970's and was #253 in 2015. Melissa means "bee." Tessa is a short form of Theresa, meaning "to harvest." Tessa was #209 in 2015.

Acacia, Aisha, Alicia, Ambrosia, Anastasia, Asia, Dacia, Deja, Fantasia, Felicia, Freesia, Iesha, Kadisha, Kamisha, Kasia, Keisha, Latasha, Latisha, Leticia, Marsha, Mischa, Natasha, Nisha, Patricia, Persia, Portia, Prisha, Sasha, Tanisha, Tasha, Trecia, Trisha

Although Anastasia is often connected with the Russian princess, the name is Greek, taken from the word anastasis, meaning "resurrection" or "rebirth." It has been a popular choice over time, except for a drop off the in the 1930s – 1950s when simpler names like Mary and Linda topped the charts. Anastasia was ranked #216 in 2015. If you are looking for a truly Russian moniker, try Natasha, meaning "born at Christmas." Natasha came into the top 1000 in 1965 and was ranked #666 in 2015, quite a drop from #70 in 1986. Tasha is a simplified version of Natasha. There were 15 U.S. baby girls named Tasha in 2015.

Amata, Amorita, Amrita, Anita, Arietta, Arista, Astra, Avita, Benita, Benta, Berta, Bonita, Bretta, Brietta, Brita, Britta, Calista, Carlotta, Colletta, Dakota, Delta, Desta, Donata, Donita, Etta, Evita, Ghita, Greta, Fausta, Fleta, Jetta, Joletta, Juanita, Krista, Loretta, Magenta, Marta, Oleta, Renata, Rita, Roberta, Sunita, Trista, Valetta, Venita, Violeta, Vita

Two unique names to consider are Brietta and Arietta. Brietta is a Celtic variation of Briar, meaning "thorny bush of wild roses." Arietta refers to the musical term, literally meaning "little aria." Neither have been in the top 1000. Less than 5 baby girls were named Brietta in 2015 and only 14 were named Arietta. A fun choice that I've always admired is Magenta. Its origins stem from a town in Italy, but obviously is now mostly linked with the vivid color. 7 U.S. baby girls were named Magenta in 2015.

Agatha, Aretha, Diantha, Martha, Samantha, Tabitha

Martha is a pretty name with Biblical history. It is of Aramaic origin, and means "lady." While slowly being used less over time, it was still ranked inside the top 1000 U.S. baby girl names at #791 in 2015. If you want to be truly unique, take a look at Diantha. This Greek name means "divine flower." Less than 5 U.S. baby girls were named this in 2015.

Ava, Aviva, Dova, Doveva, Eva, Geneva, Minerva, Nova, Reva, Silva, Tikva, Tiva, Tova

Hurray for –va names! They are a favorite of mine. If you are going the more traditional route, try Ava or Eva. They are both variations of Eve, meaning "life" and are very popular right now (Ava #4 and Eva #75 in 2015). What about Minerva (Latin, meaning "the mind")? Minerva was the Roman Goddess of wisdom and a powerful witch in Harry Potter. 51 U.S. baby girls were named Minerva in 2015.

Alexa, Lexa

Alexa first made its debut in the top 1000 girl names in the U.S. in 1973. In 2015, it jumped to #32, its best rank ever. Only 42 baby girls were named Lexa in the U.S. in 2015. Alexa and Lexa are forms of Alexander, meaning "defender of mankind."

Aliya, Amaya, Anya, Baya, Brea, Chaya, Dania, Daya, Drea, Enya, Freya, Gardenia, Gaia, Haya, Jalaya, Katya, Kaya, Maya, Neveah, Nya, Raya, Samaya, Sariah, Sequoia, Shania, Shreya, Sonya, Svea, Talya, Tanya, Vanya, Zendaya, Zoya

Have you considered Baya (meaning "berry" in Spanish)? 12 U.S. baby girls were named Baya in 2015. There were 14 named Beya and 5 named Beyah. I also like Haya, since it's my childhood friend's name. Haya is a Hebrew name meaning "life." Haya is also Arabic and means "modest." 69 U.S. baby girls were named Haya in 2015.

Aranza, Briza, Carenza, Claritza, Eliza, Esperanza, Faiza, Feliza, Itza, Leeza, Liza, Louisa, Maritza, Reza

Maritza ("of the sea") and Esperanza ("hope") are two beautiful Spanish names. Of the two, Esperanza is the more popular, making it back into the top 1000 in 2015 at #926. There were 207 baby girls named Maritza in 2015, placing it just outside of the top 1000.

Girl names with an "ee-a" sound

Abria, Acadia, Adelia, Adria, Alandria, Alaria, Alenia, Alexandria, Alexia, Althea, Ambria, Amelia, Anaya, Angelia, Antonia, Arcadia, Aria, Astoria, Atalia, Audria, Aurelia, Belvia, Bethelia, Bria, Calia, Cambria, Cascadia, Cassia, Cecilia, Celia, Christia, Claudia, Cordelia, Cornelia, Cynthia, Dalia, Daria, Delicia, Deloria, Dorothea, Dulcea, Emilia, Eugenia, Evia, Flavia, Gardenia, Gloria, Gia, Halia, Hestia, India, Jessenia, Jovia, Julia, Kalia, Leah, Lilia, Linnea, Lovinia, Lydia, Magnolia, Malia, Maria, Mariah, Melania, Mia, Moriah, Nadia, Natalia, Nivea, Odelia, Olivia, Ophelia, Orelia, Pia, Salvia, Shaylea, Sophia, Talia, Thea, Tia, Toria, Valeria, Victoria, Yesenia, Zariah, Zinnia

Girl names ending with –ia are very popular right now. Sophia was #1 in 2011, 2012, and 2013. Olivia has been in the top 10 since 2001 and Mia has been in the top 10 since 2009. If you are looking for a less popular, but similar sounding choice, consider Talia, which came onto the charts in 1977 and ranked #284 in 2015. Talia is Hebrew and means, "dew from heaven." Or you might look at Daria, an older name which managed to climb back into the top 1000 girl names in the U.S. from 1997-1999 before dropping off again. There were 125 U.S. baby girls named Daria in 2015. Daria means "wealthy."

Girl names with an "ay" or "i" sound

Dae, Denae, Desiree, Dulce, Esme, Faraday, Faye, Guadalupe, Ismay, Janae, Kay, Lanae, May, Mireille, Monday, Monet, Rae, Renee, Shaye, Siboney, Sunday, Tuesday, Wednesday

Considering a name ending with an –ay sound? What about Desiree? It's French and means "desired." Desiree made it into the top 1000 U.S. girl names in 1954 at #975 and jumped all the way up to #308 the following year. In 2015 Desiree fell to #813, its lowest rank since 1954. What about Dulce? In the U.S. it's most often pronounced DOOL-seh, but can also be pronounced DUL-chay. Dulce is Latin and means "sweet." In 2015 Dulce ranked #663 for U.S. baby girl names.

Bly, July, Lorelei, Sarai, Sky

An interesting tidbit about the name Lorelei: It's a German name meaning "alluring temptress." The name is from a legend about a beautiful siren on the Rhine River that lured sailors to their deaths. Lorelei was #448 for U.S. girl names in 2015. Sky was #773 in 2015, but the more popular spelling is Skye #385. There were also 72 baby girls named Skyy. Sky is also used as a boy name. There were 81 baby boys named Sky in 2015.

Girl names with an "ee" sound

Abby, Bea, Bebe, Darby, Debbie, Gabby, Libby, Phoebe, Ruby, Shelby, Selby, Tabby

Phoebe has the interesting history of being a Biblical name, from Greek mythology, and used by Shakespeare. Phoebe (pronounced FEE-BEE) means "brilliant" or "shining one." Phoebe was #217 in 1880 and #287 in 2015. I'm a little bit partial to Ruby. This gem name was very popular in the 1910s and 1920s and is moving up the charts again. It ranked #83 in 2015.

Addie, Andy, Birdie, Brandy, Cassidy, Cindy, Dee, Dodie, Elodie, Goldie, Haddie, Heidi, Indy, Jody, Judy, Kennedy, Lindy, Maddie, Mandy, Melody, Mendi, Mindy, Sadie, Sandy, Rhapsody, Tandy, Trudy, Wendy, Windy

Cassidy can be a girl or boy's name, though it's primarily used for girls these days. In 2015 it was #257 for baby girls in the U.S. Cassidy is Gaelic and means "curly haired." Sadie (a form of Sarah, meaning "Princess") was ranked #74 in 1880 and was #52 in 2015.

Sophie, Taffy

Sophie is not as popular as Sophia, which dropped from #1 to #2 in 2015. This may be a nice feature for parents who don't want a top 10 pick. Sophie was #104 in 2015.

Angie, Maggie, Margie

Maggie, a form of Margaret (meaning "pearl") has held steady over the years. It was at #46 in 1880 and has never dropped out of the top 1000 U.S. baby girl names. Its lowest point was in 1970 at #806. Maggie was #241 in 2015.

Sookie, Nikki, Jackie

Using the full name seems to be the more popular choice right now. Nikki was not in the top 1000 vs Nicole at #152 in 2015. Jackie was not in the top 1000 either. Jacqueline was #258 in 2015. 8 U.S. baby girls were named Sookie in 2015.

Ainsley, Ally, Amelie, Amberleigh, Arlie, Ashley, Avalea, Avonlea, Bailey, Berkley, Bexley, Blakely, Beverly, Billie, Brynlee, Callie, Carly, Carolee, Cecily, Charly, Cohlee, Dolly, Ellie, Emily, Ensley, Evalea, Everlee, Finley, Galilee, Hadley, Hallie, Hartley, Hayley, Henley, Hilly, Holly, Islee, Jaylee, Jolie, Julie, Kaylee, Keeley, Kelly, Kenley, Kensley, Kimberly, Kinley, Kinsley, Kirrily, Kylee, Langley, Leslie, Lily, Lindley, Marilee, Marley, Maylee, Mckinley, Melly, Miley, Millie, Molly, Natalie, Nathalie, Nellie, Nolee, Novalie, Oakley, Ollie, Orli, Paisley, Pearlie, Pemberley, Polly, Presley, Raylee, Riley, Rosalie, Sally, Seeley, Shaylee, Shelly, Shirley, Tali, Tenley, Thessaly, Tilly, Tinsley, Tylee, Valley, Waverly

Ainsley is an Old English/Scottish surname, meaning "One's own meadow." Some think of it as a fresh version of Ashley. Ainsley hit the U.S. rankings for girl names in 2001 at #482 and was #339 in 2015. Even newer? Oakley, which rose into the top 1000 U.S. baby girl names in the #928 spot in 2013 and was #611 in 2015. Besides the Annie Oakley connection, the name means "Oak tree grove."

Amy, Bellamy, Demi, Emmy, Jaime, Jessamy, Kami, Mimi, Naomi, Remy, Romy, Sammy, Stormy, Tammy

While not in the top 1000, Bellamy is a nice choice. Bellamy is from Old French, meaning "fair friend." 183 U.S. girls were named Bellamy in 2015. Amy is also from Old French and means "beloved." Amy peaked in the mid 1970s but is still highly popular at #158 in 2015. Naomi is a Hebrew/Biblical name meaning "pleasant," and has been steadily trending upward since the 1990s. Naomi reached #77 in 2015.

Albany, Bethany, Bonnie, Briony, Brittney, Connie, Courtney, Dagny, Daphne, Delaney, Destiny, Ebony, Ethne, Ginnie, Harmony, Hermoine, Imani, Ione, Janie, Jenny, Joni, Journey, Laney, Lani, Leilani, Leonie, Linnie, Marnie, Melanie, Minnie, Nalani, Nani, Penny, Rainey, Ronni, Stephanie, Sunny, Sydney, Tawny, Tierney, Tiffany, Tony, Whitney, Winnie

Have you considered Briony? This is a top 100 British name for baby girls, but very uncommon in the U.S. Briony means "climbing plant" and is sometimes spelled Bryony. Only 9 U.S. baby girls were named Briony in 2015. An up and coming name in the group is Journey, which popped into the top 1000 lists in 1999. Journey was #274 in 2015, and her alternate spelling, Journee, was not far behind at #377. Leilani, a beautiful Hawaiian name meaning "heavenly flower," continues to trend. Leilani was #178 in 2015.

Chloe, Joey, Joy, Zoey

Chloe was a popular choice even in 1880 at #367. In 2015 it was #17 for U.S. baby girls. Chloe is Greek and means "blooming." Zoey is also Greek, and means "life." Zoey was #23 in 2015 (The alternate spelling Zoe was #33).

Penelope, Poppy

In Greek mythology, Penelope waited patiently for her husband Odysseus to return. Penelope means "thread" or "web" and jumped from #125 in 2012 to #34 in 2015. Poppy has never been in the top 1000 girls names in the U.S. There were 257 U.S. baby girls named Poppy in 2015. However, Poppy is a top 100 name in England, Wales, Ireland and Scotland.

Adishree, Amari, Ari, Aubrey, Audrey, Avery, Bree, Cambry, Carrie, Ellery, Embry, Emery, Devory, Florie, Glory, Hillary, Irie, Ivy, Ivory, January, Jory, Kari, Keri, Kyrie, Landry, Laurie, Laree, Mabry, Mallory, Marjorie, Mary, Miri, Neri, Nori, Perry, Rory, Rosemary, Story, Shari, Shree, Siri, Suri, Teri, Tori, Valarie, Zuri,

Embry (an English surname meaning "work rule") might work as a happy medium between the ever popular Emma and Aubrey. Embry has never been in the top 1000 U.S. baby names. There were 51 baby girls and 15 baby boys named Embry in the U.S. in 2015. Landry, meaning "land ruler" is another nice-sounding unisex English surname. There were 260 boys and 297 girls named Landry in 2015. That puts the rankings at #858 for boys and #918 for girls.

Annecy, Bessie, Casey, Cassie, Cece, Cecily, Chelsea, Chrissy, Circe, Dacey, Darcy, Delancy, Elsie, Gracie, Jaycee, Jessie, Josie, Kelsey, Lacy, Lancy, Legacy, Lexi, Lucy, Macy, Mercy, Missy, Rossi, Stacy, Tacey, Tracy, Tressie

Lucy is from the Latin name Lucia, meaning "light." Lucy is highly popular in England both historically, #36 in 1880 and was top 30 in England in 2014. Similarly, Lucy was #44 in the U.S. in 1880 and #55 in 2015. Legacy is a word name (like Journey) that is gaining ground, but is still very unique. 20 U.S. baby girls were named Legacy in 2000. In 2015 there were 163 baby girls and 59 baby boys named Legacy.

Alesti, Amity, Arrietty, Betsy, Betty, Binty, Calamity, Clarity, Dottie, Dusty, Ettie, Felicity, Hattie, Infinity, Kitty, Kirstie, Kristy, Lettie, Liberty, Lottie, Misty, Natty, Netty, Parvati, Patty, Serenity, Shanti, Trinity, Vashti, Verity, Zetty

There are several virtue baby names above, such as Amity, Infinity, Liberty, Serenity, Trinity and Verity. The most popular of these is Serenity at #71 in 2015, followed by Trinity at #130 and Liberty at #558. Never in the top 1000, Amity, means "friendship" or "harmony" and has two interesting pop culture references that parents might want to be aware of. Amity is the name of one of the factions in the YA best-seller, Divergent, and is also the first name of the author of The Forgotten Man, a book that has shaped modern conservative thinking. There were 37 U.S. baby girls named Amity in 2015.

Dorothy, Wealthy

These two are decidedly older names and one of them is making a comeback. Dorothy, meaning "gift of God," popped back onto U.S. lists in 2011 and was at #714 in 2015. Less than 5 baby girls were named Wealthy in 2015.

Devi, Evie, Ivy, Jovi, Livy, Savy, Stevie, Sylvie, Vivi

Ivy has enjoyed a stable popularity over time. 1946 is the only year Ivy did not make the top 1000 baby girl names. In 2015 Ivy ranked #129. Devi (pronounced DEV-ee) is an Indian/Sanskrit name meaning "divine" or "goddess." Devi has never been in the top 1000 U.S. baby girl names.18 baby girls were name Devi in 2015.

Dixie, Lexi

Have you thought about Dixie for your little Southern Belle? Dixie, mostly considered a place name for the American South, is French and means "tenth." Dixie was #944 in 2015 for U.S. baby girl names. Lexi was ranked #308 and Lexie was #713 in 2015. Lexi is short feminized version of Alexander ("defender of man").

Daisy, Izzy, Kenzie, Kinsey, Lindsey, Lizzy, Mackenzie, Maisie, Mitzi, Posey, Rosie, Tansy

Considering flower names? Rosie reached the top 1000 in 2013 after staying out for 30 years and was #774 in 2015. Daisy was #183 in 2015. Posey and Tansy are more unique, but with the same cheerful quality as the other two. There were 41 U.S. baby girls named Posey and 6 named Tansy in 2015.

Girl names ending with an "o" or "oo" sound

Calisto, Calypso, Cameo, Cho, Cleo, Coco, Dido, Doe, Echo, Harlow, Indigo, Isabeau, Juno, Keiko, Margo, Marlowe, Meadow, Shiloh, Snow, Sparrow, Willow, Winslow

Don't you just love names ending with an 'o' sound? There are lots of nature options like Meadow, which came into the top 1000 baby girl names in 2001. Meadow was #677 in 2015. Willow is steadily rising, hitting #111 in 2015. Have you ever heard the name Isabeau (pronounced IZ-ah-bow)? It is a French form of Isabel, meaning "pledged to God" and was popular in the Middle Ages. 19 U.S. baby girls were named Isabeau in 2015.

Blue, Drew, Rue, Sue

Rue means "regret" in English and "street" in French. It's also an herb and a beloved character in The Hunger Games. There were 31 U.S. baby girls named Rue in 2014 and 26 in 2015. Drew used to be almost exclusively a boy's name, but is now accepted for either sex. There were 212 U.S. baby girls named Drew in 2015 compared to 885 baby boys given the name.

Girl names ending with a "ch" sound

Blanche, March, Peach

Blanche hasn't been in the top 1000 since 1964. Less than 5 U.S. baby girls were named Blanche in 2015. Blanche is a French name meaning "white" and started as a nickname for fair blondes. March and Peach were not listed for 2015.

Girl names ending with a "d" or "g" sound

Adelaide, Astrid, Bathilde, Brigid, Diamond, Emerald, Enid, Ermengarde, Gertrude, Gilead, Holland, Ingrid, Ireland, Jade, Kayland, Marigold, Maud, Mildred, Orchid, Rosalind, Rosamund, Rosebud, Ryland, Sade, Scotland, Sigrid, Soledad, Winifred

There are a lot of pretty names above. I like Marigold, a flower name with a sunny disposition. 66 U.S. baby girls were named Marigold in 2015. The gem name Jade is enjoying some popularity these days. It came into the top 1000 U.S. baby girl names in 1975 and was #126 in 2015. But let's not overlook the other green gem. Emerald was in the top 1000 U.S. baby girl names from 1991 to 2002. 193 U.S. baby girls were named Emerald in 2015. Emerald might be a nice alternative to Emma if you're looking for something more unique.

Meg, Peg

Meg and Peg are usually nicknames, but 19 U.S. baby girls were named Meg in 2015. Less than 5 baby girls were named Peg in 2015.

Girl names ending with an "ing" or "j" sound

Aisling, Blessing, Darling, Spring, Starling

Only 21 U.S. baby girls were named Spring in 2015. Aisling (pronounced ASH-ling) is an Irish/Gaelic name meaning "dream." 48 U.S. baby girls were named Aisling in 2015.

Madge, Paige, Sage

Paige is an English name, meaning "attendant" and has been in the top 1000 since 1952. In 2015, it was #140. Sage came into the top 1000 in 1993. Sage means "wise one" and also originates from the fragrant herb of the same name. In 2015, Sage was #370 for U.S. baby girls (Saige was #711). Sage is also a baby boy name, ranking #649 on the boy's list.

Girl names ending with a "k" or "l" sound

Angelique, Blake, Brooke, Dominique, Kendrick, Lake, Lark, Lilac, Lyric, Monique, Skylark

Brooke has been in the top 200 since 1976. It was #150 in 2015. Brooke is Old English and means "brook" or "stream." Lake has a similar meaning, but is very much less mainstream, pardon the pun. 48 U.S. baby girls and 64 U.S. baby boys were named Lake in 2015. Blake (Old English, meaning "black") used to be almost exclusively given to baby boys and is still a popular boy name (#96 in 2015 for U.S. baby boys). Starting in 1990, the name made it into the top 1000 list for girls. It was #423 in 2015.

Abigail, Adele, Angel, Annabelle, April, Arabelle, Ariel, Arielle, Avielle, Avril, Azul, Belle, Beryl, Brielle, Bristol, Camille, Campbell, Carmel, Carole, Cecile, Chanel, Chantal, Christabel, Clarabelle, Coral, Criselle, Crystal, Danielle, Dayle, Elle, Estelle, Ethel, Gabrielle, Gail, Giselle, Gretel, Hazel, Hazelle, Isabelle, Isobel, Itzel, Janelle, Jewel, Jill, Joelle, Jonquil, Kendall, Lashelle, Laurel, Leisel, Lucille, Marcelle, Marisol, Mabel, Marielle, Meryl, Michelle, Mirabel, Miral, Mirielle, Muriel, Nell, Nicole, Noelle, Opal, Pearl, Rachel, Raquel, Rochelle, Roselle, Sabelle, Sheryl, Sibyl, Soleil, Sorrel, Zoelle

There are many beautiful and diverse names ending with the –el sound. Abigail is a Biblical name meaning, "the father's joy." Abigail became popular in the 1970s and has skipped up the charts, reaching #7 in 2015. Avril is a French form of April, and means "second" as the old calendar started with March. About a dozen U.S. baby girls were named Avril every year until Avril Lavigne's first album in 2002. From 2003 on, 100+ baby girls were named Avril every year. In 2015 there were 129. Gabrielle is a French name meaning, "God is my strength" and was #205 in 2015. The shortened version, Brielle, is even more popular at #128 in 2015. Isabelle is a Spanish form of Elizabeth and means "God is my oath." Isabelle, and all her close relatives are popular with Isabella #5, Isabelle #94, Isabel #149, Isabela #769 and Izabella #234 for 2015.

Girl names ending with an "m" sound

Anthem, Bethlehem, Blossom, Chrysanthemum, Dream, Emme, Gem, Kim, Miriam, Salem, Sam, Tam, Tatum

Miriam, a Hebrew/Biblical name that can mean "bitter," "rebellious" or "wished for child," was #294 in 2015. Tatum is English and means "Tate's homestead." Tatum has been in the top 1000 U.S. baby girl names since 1994 and was #410 in 2015. Although unisex names usually start as boy names, in this case Tatum started as a girl's name and became popular with boys too. Tatum showed up in the top 1000 U.S. baby boy names in 2010 and was #590 in 2015.

Girl names ending with an "n" sound (single syllable names first)

Anne, Brynn, Dawn, Fawn, Fern, Finn, Flynn, Gwen, Gwyn, Jan, Jane, Jean, Jen, Joan, June, Lane, Lynn, Nan, Prynn, Quinn, Rain, Roane, Sloane, Sun, Wren, Wynn

Have you considered Brynn? The name is Welsh and means "hill." Brynn was #259 in 2015. What about a nature name? Wren made it into the top 1000 for the first time in 2013 at #807 and was #712 in 2015. There were also 93 baby girls named Rain in 2015.

Adrianne, Arianne, Bethann, Betsan, Brianne, Cheyenne, Corianne, Deanne, Diane, Floriane, Georgianne, Gillian, Joanne, Julianne, Kianne, Leanne, Lillian, Luanne, Lucianne, Marianne, Oceane, Rianne, Roseann, Roxanne, Susan, Susanne, Tessanne, Vivian

Cheyenne is an American Indian name meaning, "unintelligible speakers" and is also the capital of Wyoming. In 2015, Cheyenne was #347. Lillian, a Latin name meaning "lily" was very popular in the early 1900s and has made a huge comeback, sitting at #26 in 2015.

Robin

Robin is a unisex name that has not been in the top 1000 U.S. baby girl names since 2004. In 2015 there were 223 baby girls and 188 baby boys named Robin. Parents are leaning toward its trendier cousin Wren, #712 in 2015, but are still overlooking Lark (only 37 baby girls were named Lark in 2015).

Gretchen

Gretchen (a form of Margaret) is German and means "pearl." The name peaked in the 1970s and dropped off the list after 2009. In 2015 there were 160 U.S. baby girls named Gretchen.

Arden, Berdine, Camden, Eden, Geraldine, Golden, Hayden, Iden, Jayden, Jordan, Linden, London Nadine, Sheridan

Arden is a Celtic place name meaning "high" and was a top 1000 U.S. baby boy name until the 1960s. It's now trending for baby girls, hitting the top 1000 for girls in 2015 at #912 for the first time since 1931. Eden, the Biblical garden of our first parents, came into the top 1000 in 1986. In 2015, Eden ranked #156. London, another place name (though not nearly as heavenly) is also trending up. London was #105 in 2015. That's quite a jump from #919 in 1999.

Brienne, Julienne, Lucienne, Vivienne

Vivienne is the French form of Vivian (Latin, meaning "life") and both are trending right now. Vivian, was #95 in 2015. Vivienne dropped out of the top 1000 in 1930, but came back at #531 in 2009. In 2015 it was #233. A big part of the comeback for Vivienne was due to Brad Pitt and Angelina Jolie. They chose Vivienne in 2008 for one of their twins.

Delphine, Josephine, Persephone, Seraphine

Josephine (the feminine version of Joseph, meaning "God increases") is by far the most popular of the above names. Josephine has always been in the top 500 of U.S. baby girl names since they began charting in 1880. In 2015, Josephine was #131. The angelic name Seraphine is the French form of the Hebrew word, meaning "burning ones." There were 25 baby girls named Seraphine in 2015.

Kerrigan, Logan, Megan, Morgan, Reagan, Teagan

Although Kerrigan (an Irish name meaning "dark hair") is listed many places as a boy's name, it's used more for baby girls in the U.S. than for boys. In 2015, 98 baby girls and 5 baby boys were named Kerrigan. With the exception of Megan, all of these are unisex names. Here is the breakdown for 2015: Logan #394 for girls, #14 for boys. Morgan #120 for girls, #674 for boys. Reagan #99 for girls, #991 for boys. Teagan #228 for girls, dropped out of top 1000 for boys for the first time since 2004.

Imogen, Imogene

What started as a misprint from Shakespeare (Innogen became Imogen) is now a popular name in Britain. Imogen (meaning "maiden") was #49 in England in 2014, and although only given to 141 baby girls in the U.S. in 2015, many think it will make a big jump in the next few years. Imogene is the Americanized version of Imogen, and was in the top 1000 U.S. baby girl names until 1955. In 2015, 33 U.S. baby girls were named Imogene.

Laken, Larkin

Larkin is an Irish surname meaning "rough" or "fierce." It's used for both boys and girls. In 2015, 81 U.S. baby girls and 42 U.S. baby boys were named Larkin. Laken, a variation of Lake, made it into the top 1000 U.S. baby girl names from 1990-1995. It too is a unisex name. In 2015, 133 girls and 107 boys were named Laken.

Abilene, Adeline, Adelyn, Aileen, Aislin, Angeline, Apolline, Arlene, Avalon, Aveline, Aylin, Baelyn, Brilynn, Brooklyn, Carlin, Caroline, Carolyn, Celine, Charlene, Charlyn, Coraline, Coralyn, Cymbeline, Darlene, Eileen, Ellen, Emmaline, Emmalyn, Evangeline, Evelyn, Faline, Gracelyn, Gwendolyn, Halen, Harlan, Hartlyn, Helene, Helen, Isabelline, Jacqueline, Jazlyn, Jaylene, Jennilyn, Jessalyn, Jocelyn, Jolene, Kayleen, Katelyn, Kathleen, Luellen, Madeline, Madelyn, Magdalen, Magdalene, Mandolin, Marilyn, Marlene, Nadalyn, Nicoleen, Opaline, Pauline, Raelene, Raelyn, Rosaline, Rosalyn, Selene, Shaelyn, Skylen

The most popular of the -lyn names is Evelyn at #15 in 2015. If you think of Evelyn as a form of Eve, the name means "life." As a French form of Aveline, it means "hazelnut." Its Latin root means "bird." Celine (the French variation of Celeste, meaning "heavenly") was in the top 1000 U.S. baby girl names from 1994 to 2005, following the career rise of Celine Dion. It made a comeback in 2012 and was #824 in 2015.

Carmen, Charmaine, Jasmine, Jessamine, Simone, Yasmin

Jasmine peaked at #23 in 1993 and 1994 after Disney's Aladdin came to theatres at the end of 1992. This beautiful flower name is still blooming in all its spelling varieties. In 2015, the rankings were as follows: Jasmine #112, Jazmine #449, Jazmin #431, Jasmin #885. Jessamine and Yasmin (#932) are also variations of Jasmine. There were 14 baby girls named Jessamine in the U.S. in 2015.

Eponine, Janine, Shannon, Rhiannon

Shannon is an Irish form of Sean, meaning "old" or "wise" and is also the name of the longest river in Ireland. Shannon was popular for both girls and boys in the U.S. in the 1970's, reaching #22 for baby girls and #94 for baby boys in 1972, but dropped out of the top 1000 in 2014. 248 U.S. baby girls were named Shannon in 2015. Rhiannon (pronounced Ree-ANN-on) is a Welsh mythological goddess of fertility. The name jumped into the top 1000 baby girl names at #593 in 1976, mainly due to Fleetwood Mac's song, 'Rhiannon'. The name stayed in the top 1000 until 2007. 118 U.S. baby girls were named Rhiannon in 2015.

Aspen, Espen

*Aspen first appeared in the top 1000 in 1993
and was #372 in 2015. Aspen is also used for
boys. There were 87 U.S. baby boys named
Aspen in 2015. Espen is Norwegian and means
"divine bear." Although traditionally a boy's
name, 9 U.S. baby girls were named Espen in
2015.*

Camryn, Clarine, Corrine, Erin, Florine, Irene,
Karen, Kathryn, Katrin, Kieran, Lauren, Leiren,
Lorraine, Maren, Maureen, Nasrin, Serene,
Severine, Sharon, Taren

*Katherine (a Greek name, meaning "pure") was
#84 in 2015. The alternate spelling, Catherine
was #179. Perhaps you might consider Serene,
meaning "tranquil." 71 U.S. baby girls were
named Serene in 2015.*

Addison, Allison, Crimson, Ellison, Emerson,
Francine, Jensine, Kennison, Madison, Mason,
Maxine, Racine, Sunshine, Tamsin, Tennyson

*I like Emerson (meaning "son of Emery") as a
unique alternative to Emma or Emily. It could
also be a nod to Ralph Waldo Emerson. Emerson
was #180 in 2015, with the spelling Emersyn at
#393. Emerson is also a popular boys name, at
#301 for boys in 2015. Speaking of baby names
inspired by famous poets, consider Tennyson
meaning "son of Dennis." There were 22 girls
and 45 boys given the name Tennyson in 2015.*

Afton, Anniston, Autumn, Brighton, Bristyn, Britton, Carrington, Christine, Clementine, Fantine, Justine, Kensington, Kirsten, Kristen, Leighton, Lexington, Payton, Tristen

With Winter trending (#549 in 2015) it's no surprise that Autumn is too. Autumn was #67 in 2015. For you die-hard Jane Austen fans, what about Brighton, the English coastal city Mrs. Bennett longed to visit? There were 147 U.S. baby boys and 102 U.S. baby girls named Brighton in 2015. Another British place name to consider is Kensington, which hit the top 1000 baby girl names in 2015 at #971.

Bevin, Devin, Haven, Heaven, Raven, Shavon, Siobhan

Haven (meaning, "a place of refuge") and Heaven are two place names (so to speak) that came into the top 1000 U.S. baby girl names rankings in the 1990s and have followed a similar path. In 2015, Haven was #330 and Heaven was #357.

Arwen, Bronwyn, Elowen, Gwen, Melwyn, Rowan

In 2015, 115 U.S. baby girls were named Arwen (Welsh, meaning "noble maiden"). Bronwyn, also Welsh, means "fair breast." There were 43 U.S. baby girls named Bronwyn in 2015. Elowen is Cornish and means "Elm." 36 U.S. baby girls were named Elowen in 2015. Rowan (Gaelic, "little red-haired one") is the most popular of these, but is even more popular as a boy's name. In 2015, Rowan ranked #219 for boys and #331 for girls.

Girl names ending with a "p" or "r" sound

Hope, Tulip

Hope continues to be a popular U.S. baby girl name, ranking #231 in 2015. 12 baby girls in the U.S. were named Tulip in 2015.

Amber, Arbor, Aster, Azure, Blair, Briar, Camber, Cher, Clover, Copper, Coriander, December, Easter, Eleanor, Ember, Esther, Ever, Eyre, Favor, Fleur, Ginger, Guinevere, Harper, Heather, Hesper, Hester, Honor, Jennifcr, Juniper, Kimber, Lavender, Lenore, Lior, Noor, November, Pepper, Pilar, Piper, Poplar, Rumer, Samaire, Samar, Sapphire, Sawyer, Saylor, September, Skipper, Skylar, Spencer, Star, Summer, Taylor, Timber, Tyler, Vesper, Winter, Zephyr

Calendar names are rarely used these days. There were 40 Decembers, 28 Septembers and 27 Novembers born in 2015. But the root of these, Ember, is shooting up the charts. Ember came into the top 1000 in 2009 and was #399 for U.S. baby girls in 2015. Ember might be a nice alternative to Amber, which peaked in 1986 at #13 and was #334 in 2015. Speaking of unique Amber alternatives, what about Azure? 35 U.S. baby girls were named this brilliant blue color in 2015. What about a sensory name like Clover, Coriander, Ginger, Lavender or Pepper? There were less than 5 baby girl Corianders in the U.S. in 2015, but there were 178 Clovers, 149 Peppers, 68 Gingers and 60 Lavenders.

Girl names ending with an "s" or "sh" sound

Agnes, Angeles, Alexis, Alice, Amaryllis, Amaris, Annalise, Avis, Beatrice, Bernice, Bess, Cadence, Candace, Caprice, Carys, Ceres, Charisse, Charlese, Clarice, Collins, Constance, Corliss, Dallas, Damaris, Denise, Deloris, Des, Dorcas, Doris, Eirlys, Elise, Eris, Essence, Eunice, Faris, Felice, Florence, Francis, Genesis, Gladys, Grace, Hollis, Iris, Isis, Janice, Jess, Joyce, Jules, Justice, Karris, Kris, Leise, Lexis, Lois, Lotus, Lourdes, Luz, Maris, Marleise, Mavis, Paris, Patience, Patrice, Phyllis, Promise, Reese, Seras, Solstice, Talise, Tavis, Temperance, Tess, Venice

Grace was a top 25 name from 1880 to 1914 and is just as popular today at #19 in 2015. If you're looking for something new, take a look at Collins (diminutive of Nicolas, meaning "victory"). Collins was given a boost by the 2009 movie, The Blind Side (the daughter's name). Collins reached the top 1000 at #959 in 2012 and was #704 in 2015. There were also 51 baby boys named Collins in 2015. Dallas still favors boys (#255 in 2015) but was ranked #562 for baby girls in 2015.

Cherish, Irish, Trish

Cherish was #943 in 2015, dropping from its high of #640 in 2007. There were 8 U.S. baby girls named Irish in 2015. There were 9 U.S. baby girls named Trish in 2015.

Girl names ending with a "t" or "th" sound

Amethyst, Annette, Antoinette, Bernadette, Bette, Bridgette, Celeste, Charlotte, Chrisette, Claudette, Colette, Cosette, Cricket, Danette, Dorrit, Dot, Garnet, Harriet, Janet, Janette, Joette, Juliette, Kat, Kate, Kit, Laurette, Lilibet, Lisette, Lynette, Margaret, Margolette, Marguerite, Merit, Millicent, Minette, Montserrat, Nanette, Nat, Nicolette, Odette, Pat, Paulette, Rosette, Scarlett, Suzette, Sonnet, Tempest, Valette, Violet, Yvette

The most popular of the t-ending names is Charlotte, a feminine form of Charles, meaning "free man." Charlotte was #9 in 2015. Scarlett is not far behind at #22 in 2015. Scarlett came into the top 1000 in 1940, following the movie release of Gone with the Wind (the book was published in 1936). The name did not have staying power until hitting the lists again in 1992 and skyrocketing.

Amaranth, Ardith, Arisbeth, Beth, Blythe, Dianthe, Edith, Elizabeth, Faith, Gwyneth, Hyacinth, Ianthe, Judith, Kerrith, Lilith, Maribeth, Meredith, Ruth, Truth

Ruth, a Hebrew/Biblical name meaning "friend," was popular 100 years ago, staying in the top 10 from 1892 until 1930. In 2015 it was #293. Elizabeth, also Hebrew/Biblical, means "pledged to God" and was also extremely popular 100 years ago, but never lost its appeal. Elizabeth was #13 in 2015 and has never ranked lower than #26. Beth, a short form of Elizabeth, dropped out of the top 1000 after 1997. There were 44 U.S. baby girls named Beth in 2015.

Girl names ending with a "v" sound

Clove, Dove, Eve, Genevieve, Liv, Love, Maeve, Neve, Olive

Eve (Hebrew, meaning "life") ranked #476 in 2015. Genevieve, in the U.S. pronounced GEN-uh-veev, was #182 in 2015. The name means either "white wave" or "tribal woman" depending on its Germanic or Celtic roots. Olive is trending again. A top 100 name in 1900, Olive popped back onto the list in 2007 and was #264 in 2015.

Girl names ending with an "x" or "z" sound

Alex, Beatrix, Felix, Lennox

Beatrix (Latin, meaning "brings joy") was in the top 1000 U.S. baby girl names for only one year, 1883 at #760. In 2015 there were 209 U.S. baby girls named Beatrix. Lennox is a Gaelic name meaning, "Elm field." Lennox is more popular for boys (#488), but shot up in 2015, hitting the girl's top 1000 for the first time at #740.

Cruz, Dez, Eloise, Flores, Inez, Jazz, Jules, Louise, Mercedes, Primrose, Rose, Roz, Topaz

Primrose is from Middle English and means "first rose." Primrose is also a character in the book, The Hunger Games. There were 50 U.S. baby girls name Primrose in 2015. Rose is much less obscure, being a top 25 name from 1890 until 1923. Rose was #166 in 2015, its highest rank since 1968.

Boy names ending with an "ah" sound

Alpha, Coda, Costa, Cuba, Dakota, Elijah, Ezra, Francois, Hezekiah, Hosea, Ira, Isaiah, Jedidiah, Jeremiah, Jonah, Joshua, Josiah, Judah, Lakota, Luca, Micah, Michaiah, Nehemiah, Noah, Obadiah, Peta, Renshaw, Shaw, Tacoma, Tobiah, Uriah, Zachariah, Zebediah, Zechariah

Bible names are popular choices, as shown by 2015's #1 pick, Noah ("rest" or "comfort"). The other –ah ending Bible names that were top 1000: Elijah—"Jehovah is God" #11. Ezra—"help" #92. Hezekiah—"God strengthens" #678. Isaiah—"Salvation of the Lord" #49. Jedidiah—"beloved of Jehovah" #716. Jeremiah—"appointed by God" #55. Jonah—"dove" #143. Joshua—"The Lord is salvation" #33. Josiah—"The Lord supports" #57. Judah—"praised" #235. Micah—"Who is like the Lord?" #108. Nehemiah—"comforted by God" #362. Uriah—"God is my light" #578. Zachariah—"God remembers" #422. Zechariah—"God remembers" #662.

Boy names ending in an "ay" or "oy" sound

Andre, Bay, Clay, Conway, Dante, Devante, Enrique, Felipe, Frey, Gray, Jay, Jorge, Jose, Josue, Kay, McKay, Pepe, Ray, Rene, Sanjay, Shay, Shrey, Trey

Andre, the French form of Andrew, has been in the top 1000 U.S. boy names since 1924 and ranked #279 in 2015. Dante is Latin, a short version of Durant, meaning "enduring." Dante was #322 in 2015. I like Trey, a Latin name meaning "three." Trey was #557 in 2015.

Conroy, Coy, Croix, Eloy, Elroy, Koi, Leroy, McCoy, Roy, Troy

Roy, a Gaelic name meaning "red haired," was a top 20 U.S. baby boy name in the 1890s, and still managed to make it to #536 in 2015. Troy, an Irish name meaning "foot soldier," peaked in the 1960s at #40. Which explains why my mom always wanted one boy and one girl named Troy and Lisa (Lisa was #1 for most of the 1960s). She ended up with six kids and none of us are Troy or Lisa. Troy was ranked #300 in 2015.

Boy names ending with an "ee" or "i" sound.

Alby, Colby, Crosby, Jacoby, Kirby, Kobe, Rigby, Robbie, Toby

Crosby is an Old surname, gaining new life as a fresh first name. Meaning "town near the cross," Crosby hopped into the top 1000 U.S. baby boy names in 2011 and was #576 in 2015. Toby (short for the Hebrew name Tobias, meaning "God is good") has been in use since the 1930s. It was #689 in 2015.

Archie, Jacky, Lucky, Mickey, Mikey, Ricky, Rocky

Ricky is by far the most popular of these short form names, at #584 in 2015. But it's been declining year over year since the 1980s. All of these have been declining, with the exception of Rocky, which made it back into the top 1000 U.S. baby boy in 2013 after a 5 year stint off the lists. Rocky, short for Rocco, an Italian name meaning "rest," was #927 in 2015.

Andy, Bodhi, Brady, Brody, Cody, Dee, Eddy, Freddy, Grady, Hardy, Jordy, Randy, Rudy, Teddy

Brody (a Scottish surname meaning "ditch") came into the top 1000 U.S. baby boy names in 1976, peaked in 2008 at #70 and was #105 in 2015. Its alternate spelling Brodie, was #742. Brady is Irish and means "broad-chested." Brady's peak was in 2007 at #94 and was #198 in 2013. Grady (Irish, meaning "noble") was #353 in 2015.

Alfie

There were 19 U.S. baby boys named Alfie in 2015. Compare this with England. Alfie was #13 there in 2014.

Bentley, Berkeley, Billy, Blakely, Bradley, Brantley, Brawly, Brentley, Buckley, Charlie, Conley, Daley, Farley, Finley, Grantley, Harley, Henley, Huntley, Hurley, Huxley, Kelly, Kenly, Kingsley, Lee, McKinley, Oakley, Parley, Radley, Raleigh, Ridgley, Ridley, Riley, Ripley, Rowley, Stanley, Stokley, Sully, Wesley, Wiley

The –ley names for boys are a current trend with Bentley leading the pack. Bentley (from Old English meaning "bent grass meadow") came into the top 1000 U.S. baby boy names in 2007 and was #93 in 2015. Brantley (German, meaning "firebrand") is also a new favorite, jumping onto the lists at #736 in 2010 and all the way to #121 in 2015. Kingsley also appeared in 2010, but much lower on the list. Kingsley means "king's meadow" and was #747 in 2015.

Jaime, Jeremy, Jimmy, Kwame, Laramie, Remy, Sammy, Tommy

Remy is a French name that can mean "oarsman" or "remedy" depending on whether it's derived from Remigius or Remedius. Remy was also the name of the endearing rat in Disney's Ratatouille in 2007. Perhaps that's why it jumped into the top 1000 U.S. baby boy names in 2009. It was #520 in 2015 (Remy made it into the top 1000 for girls in 2014 and was #847 in 2015). Laramie is also French and means "canopy of leafy boughs." This name is equally used for boys and girls. There were 21 baby girls and 25 baby boys named Laramie in 2015.

Anthony, Antony, Armani, Benny, Danny, Denny, Donny, Gianni, Giovanni, Johnny, Kenny, Lonnie, Manny, Rodney, Romney, Ronnie, Rooney, Sidney, Sonny, Tierney, Tony, Vinny

In the top 1000 U.S. baby boy names since 1883, Anthony never seems to go out of style. This Latin name means "priceless" and was #25 in 2015. Tony, the short form of Anthony was #504 in 2015. Giovanni, the Italian version of John, meaning "God is Gracious" is also popular right now. Giovanni was ranked #130 in 2015 (Giovani was #791 and the short form, Gianni was #564).

Amari, Connery, Cory, Curry, Destry, Dimitri, Dory, Embry, Gary, Gregory, Guthrie, Harry, Henry, Humphrey, Jamari, Jeffry, Jerry, Jory, Landry, Larry, Montgomery, Murray, Perry, Rory, Terry, Zachary

Destry is a French name meaning "war horse." You might know the 1939 western, Destry Rides Again. There were 12 U.S. baby boys named Destry in 2015. Gregory, meaning "watchful," is a Greek name popular with Popes in the Catholic Church. Gregory was top 100 from 1945 to 1996 and #346 in 2015.

Alexei, Casey, Clancy, Dempsey, Dusty, Jesse, Pacey, Percy, Quincy, Rusty

Jesse was a top 150 name until 2013 and fell to #178 in 2015. Jesse is Hebrew and means "gift." Pacey is an English surname that is rarely used. There were 16 baby boys and 15 baby girls named Pacey in the U.S. in 2015. Quincy, Latin for "fifth," was #599 in 2015. There were also 146 girls named Quincy.

Coty, Monte, Rafferty, Timothy

Coty is French and means "riverbank." There were only 18 U.S. baby boys named Coty in 2015. I like Rafferty. This Irish name means "wielder of prosperity" and is catching on in England and Wales. There were 12 U.S. baby boys named Rafferty in 2015. Timothy is a Greek name that means "to honor God" and was top 25 from 1955-1982. Timothy was #147 in 2015.

Avi, Covey, Davy, Harvey, Ravi

Avi (pronounced ah-VEE) is the short form of several Hebrew names and means "father." It reached the top 1000 in 2015 at #946. There were also 37 baby girls named Avi in the U.S. in 2015. Ravi (pronounced RAH-vee) is a Hindi name meaning "sun." There were 47 baby boys named Ravi in the U.S. in 2015.

Dewey, Huey, Joey, Louie, Maui

Joey, the short form of Joseph ("God will increase"), can be used for either girls or boys, but is currently more popular for boys. There were 314 baby boys and 95 baby girls named Joey in the U.S. in 2015. What about Maui? This island name can also be used for boys or girls. There were 6 boys named Maui in 2014, but less than 5 in 2015. 7 girls were named Maui in the U.S. in 2015.

Ozzie, Ramsey

I'm a little partial to Ramsey, a Scottish name that means, "from Ram's Island." Ramsey was in the top 1000 for most of the 1980s, and a few times before and after. There were 129 baby boys and 83 baby girls name Ramsey in the U.S. in 2015. 56 U.S. baby boys were named Ozzie in 2015.

Eli, Guy, Kai, Levi, Malachi, Matai, Mekhi, Mordecai, Nicolai, Sky, Sly, Ty

Eli and Levi are two Biblical names that are hitting new heights with expectant parents. Eli means "high, ascended" and was #53 in 2015. Levi means "joining" and was #42 in 2015. Mekhi (pronounced meh-KYE) is a modern play on the name Michael, and was brought into the mainstream by actor Mekhi Phifer (ER, 8 Mile). Mekhi made the top 1000 U.S. baby boy names in 1998 and was #635 in 2015.

Boy names ending with an "o" or "oo" sound (single syllable "o" names first)

Beau, Joe, Lowe, Moe, Rowe

Beau is French and means "handsome." Beau was #203 in 2015. Joe (short for Joseph, a Hebrew name meaning "He will add") was #596 in 2015. This is a major downtrend considering Joe was #20 in 1880 and stayed in the top 100 until 1970.

Nebo

Nebo is a Biblical name that means "prophet" and is rarely used. Nebo was not listed in 2015, meaning less than 5 babies received the name.

Enrico, Francisco, Franco, Jericho, Mako, Marco, Mico, Nico, Rico, Rocco, Roscoe

Nico, short for Nicolas and Nicodemus, first appeared in the top 1000 U.S. baby boy names in 1988 and continues upward. Nico was #464 in 2015. If you're looking for a name ready for a comeback, consider Roscoe (Norse, meaning "from the deer forest"). Roscoe was in the top 1000 from 1880 until the 1970s and then disappeared. There were 71 U.S. baby boys named Roscoe in 2015.

Aldo, Alfredo, Armando, Brando, Eduardo, Fernando, Lando, Leandro, Leonardo, Ludo, Orlando, Renaldo, Ricardo, Waldo

Armando became a permanent fixture in the top 1000 in 1909 and was #413 in 2015. Armando is Germanic and means "soldier," but also has Spanish and Italian origins. Leonardo is running up the top 1000 chart, hitting #103 in 2015. Leonardo is an Italian/Spanish version of Leonard, meaning "lion-hearted." The short form, Leo, is also trending at #91 in 2015.

Diego, Hugo, Inigo, Jago, Santiago

Diego has taken a leap in the past 10 years, thanks to Dora's adventurous, animal-rescuing cousin. Diego topped out at #56 in 2006 and was #124 in 2015. Diego is the Spanish version of James, meaning "supplanter." Santiago, Spanish for "Saint James" is another name on the upswing. It moved from the #500s in the 1990s to #127 in 2015.

Antonio, Ario, Dario, Elio, Eliseo, Elvio, Emilio, Eugenio, Ezio, Geo, Giorgio, Gregorio, Horatio, Ignacio, Indio, Julio, Leo, Lucio, Mario, Mateo, Neo, Rio, Romeo, Sergio, Silvio, Theo, Valencio, Vencentio

Neo (Greek, meaning "new") was rarely used until The Matrix came out in 1999. The following year there were 116 baby boys given the name Neo. There were 80 U.S. baby boys named Neo in 2015. Romeo, Shakespeare's romantic hero, is making a comeback, jumping from #975 in 1996 to #377 in 2015. Romeo is Latin and means "pilgrim to Rome." Theo is short for Theodore and means "divine gift." Theo jumped back into the top 1000 in 2010 after being off for sixty-five years and was #408 in 2015.

Angelo, Apollo, Arlo, Carlo, Marcello, Marlow, Milo, Pablo, Paulo, Rollo, Shiloh, Winslow

Apollo, the son of Zeus in Greek mythology, came into the top 1000 U.S. baby boy names for the first time in 2012. Apollo was #751 in 2015. Marcello (pronounced Marchello) is an Italian form of Marcellus, meaning "young warrior." Marcello has not been in the top 1000 since 1982, but it's getting close. There were 155 U.S. baby boys named Marcello in 2015.

Cosmo, Mossimo

Cosmo is an Italian and Greek name meaning "order" and "beauty." It's hard not to associate it with Seinfeld's Cosmo Kramer, but there were 30 baby boys in the U.S. named Cosmo in 2015. Mossimo was not listed for 2015, meaning less than 5 baby boys were named this. Mossimo is Italian and means "the first" or "the greatest." That's a lot to live up to.

Alvino, Bruno, Emiliano, Gino, Luciano, Maximiliano, Santino, Stephano

Gino barely dropped out of the top 1000 in 2015. There were 186 U.S. baby boys named Gino in 2015. The name is short for several different Italian names including Giovanni and Eugenio. Santino is gaining popularity. Santino came into the top 1000 in 2002 and was #608 in 2015. Santino means "little saint."

Alejandro, Alessandro, Alexandro, Arturo, Cairo, Ciro, Elisandro, Genaro, Jethro, Leandro, Lisandro, Maro, Miro, Monroe

Alejandro is the Spanish form of Alexander, meaning "defender of mankind." Alejandro has been solidly in the top 1000 since 1920 and was #180 in 2015. Cairo (pronounced KYE-ro) is the capital of Egypt and also means "victorious" in Arabic. Cairo made it to the top 1000 for the first time in 2015 at #941.

Alfonso, Kelso

*Many parents have fond memories of Alfonso
Ribeiro as Carlton on The Fresh Prince of Bel-Air,
but Alfonso has been a popular name since the
1800's. It was #792 in 2015. Alfonso is a
combination of two words meaning "noble" and
"ready" in Old German. Kelso also has a TV
connection, being a main character played by
Ashton Kutcher on That '70s Show. Kelso is a
Scottish place name. There were 10 U.S. baby
boys named Kelso in 2015.*

Cato, Christo, Cuarto, Ernesto, Otto, Vito

*Cato is a Latin name meaning "wise." There
were 23 U.S. baby boys named Cato and 47
named Kato in 2015. When I hear Cato I think of
Kato Kaelin, the O.J. Simpson witness. Cato is
also the name of a tribute from The Hunger
Games. Otto, a German name meaning
"wealthy," dropped out of the top 1000 in 1974,
but came back in 2011. Otto was #543 in 2015.*

Bravo, Gustavo

*Less than 5 baby boys were named Bravo in
2015. Gustavo (a variation of Gustav, meaning
"staff of the Goths") came into the top 1000 U.S.
baby boy names in 1935 and was #529 in 2015.*

Almanzo, Alonzo, Enzo, Lorenzo, Renzo,
Vincenzo

Lorenzo (a Latin version of Laurence, meaning "laurel") has enjoyed a steady popularity, staying in the top 500 since the 1800s. It was #216 in 2015. 75 U.S. baby boys were named the short form, Renzo, in 2015. Enzo, which can be short for Lorenzo or Vincenzo, came into the top 1000 in 2003 and was #330 in 2015. Enzo is also a popular choice in Italy and France.

Aaru, Andrew, Bartholomew, Blue, Crew, Drew, Hugh, Keanu, Lou, Matthew, Montague, Stu, True

Andrew (Greek, meaning "manly") has been a top 100 choice in the U.S. since they started charting in 1880. It's hit as high as #5, and was #30 in 2015. The short form, Drew, was #363 in 2015. Matthew (Hebrew, meaning "gift of God") was #3 through most of the 1980s and 1990s. Matthew was #15 in 2015 (Mathew was #480). I considered naming our son True, but got vetoed. I still think it's a cool name. There were 56 baby boys and 38 baby girls named True in the U.S. in 2015.

Boy names ending with a "b" or "ch" sound

Jacob, Caleb, Cabe, Gabe, Jeb, Joab, Tab

Jacob (Hebrew, meaning "supplanter") was #1 from 1999 to 2012 and was #4 in 2015. Caleb is also trending at #37 in 2015 (Kaleb was #165). Caleb was a faithful spy for Moses in the Old Testament and the name means "dog" in Hebrew. Many sites will list the meaning as "whole-hearted." Both are correct.

Aldrich, Arch, Dutch, Finch, Hatch, Hutch, Mitch, Patch, Rich

None of these are commonly used today. Here are the U.S. 2015 stats: Aldrich – 9 boys, Arch – not listed, Dutch – 41 boys, Finch – 13 boys, Hatch – not listed, Hutch – 29 boys, Mitch – 16 boys, Patch – not listed, Rich – 18 boys.

Boy names ending with a "d" sound (single syllable first)

Boyd, Brad, Bud, Cade, Chad, Claude, Clyde, Creed, Dade, Ed, Field, Floyd, Ford, Grand, Herb, Hyde, Jed, Judd, Jude, Ladd, Laird, Lloyd, Ned, Quaid, Rand, Reid, Roald, Rod, Rud, Shade, Slade, Tad, Ted, Todd, Wade, Ward, Wild

Ford (English, meaning "river crossing") jumped 143 spots to reach #741 in 2015. Wade, with a very similar meaning (to wade is to move through water), was #521 in 2015.

Archibald, Arnold, Bernard, Cleveland, Clifford, Concord, Conrad, David, Delmond, Desmond, Donald, Edmund, Edward, Eland, Eldred, Elwood, Erland, Everard, Fitzgerald, Garfield, Garland, Gerald, Gerard, Gifford, Gilead, Halstead, Harold, Howard, Jared, Legend, Leland, Leonard, Leopold, Maxfield, Millard, Mohamed, Oswald, Radford, Rashad, Raymond, Redford, Redmond, Richard, Roland, Ronald, Ryland, Sharad, Sheffield, Sheppard, Sherwood, Siegfried, Sigmund, Tibold, Wayland, Whitfield, Wilfred, Willard

David ("beloved") is a Hebrew name that has always been in the top 50 in the U.S. David was #18 in 2015. Jared, meaning "he descends," is one of the few Hebrew/Biblical baby boy names that's on a downtrend. Jared was #56 in 2000 and moved down to #340 in 2015. Ryland (Old English and Irish, meaning "where rye grows") might be a good alternative to the popular Ryan (#39) or Rylan (#241). Ryland came into the top 1000 in 2003 and was #492 in 2015.

Boy names ending with an "f" or "g" sound

Cliff, Fife, Heathcliff, Joseph, Keefe, Leif, Radcliff, Ralph, Rolf, Randolph, Rudolph, Seff, Zeph

The lowest Joseph (Hebrew, "He will increase") has ever ranked was in 2011 at the #22 spot. Joseph was #21 in 2015. Randolph is a German name meaning "shield wolf." There were 44 U.S. baby boys name Randolph in 2015.

Craig, Doug, Greg, Stig, Tagg, Teague, Trigg

Craig is a Gaelic name meaning "rock, crag." Craig's popularity peaked in the 1960s at #39 and was #913 in 2015. Tagg is a short form of Taggart, an Irish name meaning "son of the priest." There were 9 U.S. baby boys named Tagg, 7 named Tag and 24 named Taggart in 2015. Teague is a Gaelic name meaning "poet." There were 48 U.S. baby boys named Teague in 2015. Teague is usually pronounced TEEg in the U.S., but can also be pronounced Teg (as in leg) or Tie-g (as in Tiger) elsewhere. Also be aware that Teague is a derogatory word used in Northern Ireland for Roman Catholics.

Boy names ending with an "ing" or "j" sound

Channing, Ewing, Fielding, Fleming, Henning, Irving, King, Kipling, Manning, Ming, Spalding, Sterling

Channing has English and Irish origins and can mean "young wolf" or "church official." Channing had its best year in 2012 at #514 and was #784 in 2015. Sterling is an English name meaning "of excellent quality." Sterling looked like it was on its way out (#899 in 2009) but jumped to #495 in 2015.

Gage, George, Ridge, Taj, Talmadge

George is a name tied to kings, presidents, and new baby royals. Although not as popular in the U.S. as it is in Europe, George was #136 in 2015. George is Greek and means "farmer." Ridge has only been in the top 1000 U.S. baby boy names three times: 1988, 1989, and 2015. It was #932 in 2015.

Boy names ending with a "k" or "l" sound

Alaric, Alec, Alric, Auric, Barak, Berk, Blake, Breck, Brick, Brock, Cedric, Chadwick, Chuck, Clark, Cormac, Deke, Derek, Dirk, Dominic, Drake, Duke, Edric, Eldric, Elek, Emrick, Enoch, Eric, Frank, Frederick, Garrick, Godric, Hank, Hawk, Hendrick, Henrik, Ike, Isaac, Jack, Jake, Jarek, Jedrek, Kendrick, Kirk, Kodiak, Link, Locke, Luke, Mac, Maddock, Malik, Marek, Mark, Maverick, Mick, Murdoch, Nick, Patrick, Rafiq, Rick, Roarke, Roderick, Sedgwick, Spike, Tarek, Tariq, Zac, Zarek, Zeke

*Eric (Old Norse, meaning "eternal ruler") peaked
in the 1970's in the U.S. at #13 and was #137 in
2015. Erik, the older spelling, was #266. Erick
was #338. Isaac is trending along with many
other Hebrew/Biblical classics. Isaac means
"laughter" and was #31 in 2015. Luke had its
best rank ever in 2015 at #28. Luke is a Biblical
name that has origins in Latin, from Lucius
meaning "light" and from the Greek Loukas
meaning "man from Lucania." Zeke is the short
form of Ezekiel (Ezekiel was #148 in 2015), a
Hebrew/Biblical name meaning "God
strengthens." Zeke popped up on the top 1000
list in 2011 and was #704 in 2015.*

Abel, Adriel, Al, Angel, Ansel, Aviel, Axel, Azriel,
Basil, Cable, Cal, Cale, Carl, Carmichael,
Castiel, Churchill, Coil, Cole, Connell, Cornell,
Cyril, Dale, Daniel, Darnel, Daryl, Dashiel, Del,
Denzel, Diesel, Doyle, Earl, Emanuel, Emil,
Errol, Ezekiel, Farrell, Gable, Gabriel, Gale,
Gavriel, Hal, Hale, Hall, Handel, Hansel,
Hershel, Howell, Ishmael, Israel, Jael, Jamal,
Joel, Khalil, Kendall, Kimball, Kyle, Lionel,
Lowell, Loyal, Lyle, Manuel, Marcel, Markel,
Marvel, Marshall, Maxwell, Mendel, Michael,
Mikael, Miguel, Mitchell, Nathaniel, Neil, Neville,
Newell, Nigel, Noble, Orville, Pascal, Paul, Pell,
Percival, Powell, Rafael, Randall, Raul,
Rockwell, Royal, Russell, Sal, Samuel, Saul,
Searle, Sol, Sorrel, Terrell, Tyrell, Virgil,
Wendell, Will, Yasiel

Axel hit the baby name charts in the U.S. in 1989, the same time Guns N' Roses was running up the music charts. Axel is a Scandinavian version of the Hebrew name Absalom, meaning "the father is peace" and is popular in Europe. Axel was #123 in the U.S. in 2015. Have you considered Cole, an English name meaning "coal-black"? Cole was #115 in 2015. Kyle (Gaelic "narrow, strait channel") peaked in 1990 at #18 and was #175 in 2015. There were also 60 baby girls named Kyle in 2015.

Boy names ending with an "m" sound

Abraham, Abram, Adam, Bingham, Braham, Brigham, Calum, Chaim, Chrome, Clem, Elam, Ephraim, Fitzwilliam, Graham, Grantham, Grisham, Hallam, Helm, Hyrum, Ingram, Isham, Jarom, Jerome, Jim, Latham, Liam, Malcolm, Mitcham, Niam, Noam, Norm, Ransom, Rohm, Rome, Sam, Shem, Tatum, Tom, William, Wyndam, Zephram

Noam is a Hebrew name with the same root as Naomi, "pleasant." It might be a nice alternative to Noah (#1 in 2015). There were 116 baby boys and 6 baby girls named Noam in the U.S. in 2015. The most well-known Noam is Noam Chomsky, a political figure with some strong views, so keep that in mind. I like Ransom, a name from Old English, meaning "son of the shield." It's also associated with rescue or deliverance. Ransom hasn't been in the top 1000 since 1930. There were 102 baby boys named Ransom in 2015. William (German, meaning "resolute protector") was #5 in the U.S. in 2015. William has never left the top 20, holding the #2 spot from 1880-1920.

Boy names ending with an "n" sound (single syllable names first)

Ben, Blaine, Bran, Braun, Cane, Chan, Chen, Crane, Dan, Dane, Dean, Don, Duane, Dunn, Fen, Finn, Flynn, Gene, Glenn, John, Juan, Ken, Keane, Lane, Len, Penn, Quinn, Ren, Rhone, Rune, Sean, Shane, Sloan, Stan, Stein, Stone, Sven, Thane, Thorne, Twain, Van, Vaughn, Vern, Wayne, Zane

Flynn (Irish, meaning "son of the red-haired") probably got a bump from Disney's Flynn Ryder, the romantic hero of Tangled. Flynn came into the top 1000 in 2011 and was #694 for U.S. baby boys in 2015 (There were 21 baby girls named Flynn in 2015). Finn is also on the rise. Finn (Irish, meaning "white, fair") came into the top 1000 in 2000 and was #209 in 2015 (There were 26 baby girls name Finn in 2015). Quinn came into the top 1000 for U.S. baby boys in 1960, but has since become a unisex name favoring baby girls. In 2015, Quinn was #354 for boys and #97 for girls.

Corbin, Esteban, Fabian, Raeburn, Reuben, Robin, Tobin

Have you considered Corbin? Corbin is an Anglo-Norman name meaning "raven" and was #221 in 2015 (Korbin was #594). Tobin is a variation of Tobias, a Hebrew name meaning "God is good." Tobin has not been in the top 1000 since 1978, but there were 127 U.S. baby boys named Tobin in 2015.

Aiken, Beacon, Brecken, Deacon, Duncan, Hawken, Joaquin, Lincoln, Ryken

Brecken, an Irish name meaning 'freckled,' came into the top 1000 U.S. baby boy names in 2011 and continues to climb. It was #725 in 2015. Lincoln is an English name meaning, "pool, lake" and is of course linked to our revered U.S. President. Lincoln also had its best year at #66 in 2015.

Adrian, Aiden, Alden, Arden, Auden, Braden, Brandon, Brendan, Brigdon, Brodin, Camden, Drayden, Edan, Eldin, Eldon, Gideon, Gordon, Grayden, Hadden, Hadrian, Hayden, Holden, Jayden, Jordan, Kayden, Landon, Layden, Lynden, Madden, Marsden, Ogden, Raiden, Reardon, Rigdon, Riordan, Roldan, Sheldon, Seldon, Viridian, Walden, Zaiden

Boy names ending in –den are very trendy right now, with Aiden and Jayden in the top 20. Aiden, an Irish name meaning "little fire" was #13 for 2015 (Ayden was #87 and Aidan was #185). Camden, a Scottish name meaning "winding valley," came into the top 1000 in 1990 and was #104 in 2015. Hayden, from Old English, means "hedged valley" and was #151 for baby boys and #190 for U.S. baby girls in 2015. Kayden was #95 in 2015, but would be a lot higher if not for all the spellings (Kaiden #140, Kaden #179, Cayden #212, Caden #192, Caiden #285).

Griffin, Hafen, Stephan

Griffin is Gaelic and means "strong lord" and is also the mythological half eagle and half lion. Griffin was #236 in 2015. Hafen is a German surname and means "potter." There were less than 5 babies named Hafen in the U.S. in 2015. Stephan (pronounced STEH-fahn) is a German name meaning "crown, garland." There were 165 U.S. baby boys named Stephan in 2015.

Brogan, Dagan, Deegan, Dugan, Eagan, Finnegan, Hagan, Hogan, Keegan, Logan, Morgan, Reagan, Rogan, Peregrine, Sagan

Deegan is an Irish name that means "black haired" and left the top 1000 after a short stint from 2008-2013. There were 171 U.S. baby boys named Deegan in 2015. Finnegan (Irish, meaning "fair") entered the top 1000 in 2005 and was #405 in 2015. Morgan is a Welsh name that means "circling sea." It ranked #674 for U.S. baby boys and #120 for girls in 2015. Rogan, an Irish name meaning "redhead," might be a nice alternative to Logan (#14 in 2015). There were 86 U.S. baby boys named Rogan in 2015.

Calhoun, Callahan, Johan

If you like the nickname Cal, you might consider Calhoun or Callahan. Both are Irish. Calhoun means "the narrow woods" and Callahan means "bright-headed." There were 12 U.S. baby boys named Calhoun in 2015 and 83 named Callahan. Johan (pronounced YOH-hahn) is a German form of John, meaning "God is gracious." Johan was ranked #553 in 2015.

Alan, Aslan, Baylen, Breylan, Colin, Cullen,
Dallin, Declan, Dylan, Elan, Elian, Franklin,
Galen, Harlon, Jaylen, Joplin, Julian, Kelan,
Kellen, Kylan, Lachlan, Malone, Marlon,
Maximilian, Milan, Nolan, Quinlan, Raylan,
Rylan, Stellan, Talan, Weylan, Wylan

*Colin is normally pronounced COLL-in, but can
also be pronounced COLE-in, as in Colin Powell.
Colin is has two origins, as a short form of
Nicolas (meaning "victory of the people") and as
a variation of the Gaelic name Cailean, meaning
"cub." Colin was #172 in 2015 and Collin was
#264. Dylan came into the top 1000 U.S. baby
boy names in 1966 and was #27 in 2015 (Dillon
was #448). Dylan is Welsh and means "son of
the sea." Kellen (Gaelic, meaning "slender") came
into the top 1000 in 1981 and was #506 in 2015.
Kellan is became the preferred spelling in 2007.
Kellan was #398 in 2015. Nolan reached a new
best at #71 in 2015. Nolan is Gaelic and means
"champion."*

Ammon, Benjamin, Bowman, Coleman,
Damien, Damon, Eamon, Freeman, Harmon,
Helaman, Herman, Jermaine, Lyman, Naman,
Neiman, Newman, Norman, Roman, Ramon,
Sherman, Simon, Solomon, Stedman, Thurman,
Tillman, Truman, Wyman, Whitman

Benjamin is another Hebrew/Biblical name trending upward. Benjamin, meaning "son of my right hand," was #10 in 2015, a new best. Naman is a Hindu name meaning "salutations" (It also has Hebrew origins – meaning "pleasant" like Naomi and Noam). There were 20 U.S. baby boys name Naman in 2015, and 16 named Naaman. Truman is an Old English name that means "loyal one," as you would expect. Truman has not been consistently in the top 1000 since the Truman Presidency, but it was #981 in 2015.

Brannon, Brennan, Canaan, Cannon, Conan, Gannon, Keenan, Lennon, Ronan, Tynan, Vernon

Canaan, pronounced KAY-nan, is a Biblical place name that reached the top 1000 in 2015 at #806. Cannon (an English word name, for the weapon) came into the top 1000 in 2003 and was #588 for U.S. baby boys in 2015. Keenan (Gaelic, meaning "ancient") peaked in 1997 at #354 and was #931 in 2015.

Caspian, Crispin, Espen

Caspian is a place name for the sea located between Asia and Russia and is also the name of a character in The Chronicles of Narnia series. There were 103 U.S. baby boys named Caspian in 2015. Crispin is Latin, meaning "curly-haired." There were 28 U.S. baby boys named Crispin in 2015. Espen is a Norwegian name meaning "divine bear." There were 37 boys named Espen in 2015.

Aaron, Baron, Byron, Cameron, Coltrane, Darren, Doran, Efrain, Heron, Iron, Jaron, Kieran, Myron, Oren, Soren, Toren, Tyrone, Warren, Zoran

Coltrane is an English name meaning "young horse." There were 13 U.S. baby boys named Coltrane in 2015. Jaron is a Hebrew name meaning "cry of rejoicing." There were 107 baby boys named Jaron in 2015 and 67 named Jaren. Kieran is an Irish name given to several Irish saints and means "little dark one." Kieran was #511 in 2015. There were also 29 U.S. baby girls name Kieran in 2015.

Anderson, Branson, Brayson, Bronson, Bryson, Cason, Carson, Chasen, Colson, Dashan, Dawson, Dennison, Dixon, Edison, Emerson, Ericson, Ferguson, Garrison, Garson, Gibson, Grayson, Hanson, Harrison, Henderson, Hobson, Hudson, Hutchison, Ibsen, Jackson, Jameson, Jason, Jefferson, Jenson, Larson, Lawson, Lucien, Mason, Maxson, Morrison, Nelson, Orson, Payson, Pierson, Reason, Saxon, Stetson, Tracen, Tyson, Wilson

The most popular of the –son names is Mason (an occupational name) at #3 in 2015. Jackson was not far behind at #17. Anderson (Scandinavian, "son of Anders") was #305 in 2015. What about Stetson? Stetson ("Steven's son" – but better known for the hat maker) was in the top 1000 U.S. baby names from 1989-1995 and came back in 2013. Stetson was #774 in 2015.

Alton, Anton, Ashton, Aston, Augustine, Austin, Axton, Barston, Barton, Bastian, Boston, Braxton, Brayton, Brexton, Brighton, Canton, Carleton, Carsten, Cashton, Charleston, Christian, Clayton, Clifton, Clinton, Colston, Colton, Constantine, Creighton, Dalton, Daxton, Dayton, Denton, Destin, Dustin, Easton, Eaton, Elton, Fenton, Fulton Halsten, Hamilton, Hampton, Heston, Horton, Houston, Hurston, Keaton, Kelton, Kenton, Kingston, Kipton, Koston, Justin, Langston, Layton, Martin, Maxton, Milton, Morton, Newton, Norton, Patton, Paxton, Payton, Preston, Quentin, Quinton, Ralston, Remington, Rustin, Seaton, Sebastian, Stanton, Stratton, Sutton, Thurston, Titan, Trenton, Tristan, Walton, Watson, Weston, Winston, Yestin

Ashton (English, meaning "ash tree town") hit its peak in 2004 at #76, but still reached #141 in 2015. There were also 189 U.S. baby girls named Ashton in 2015. I like Colton, #59 in 2015. Colton is English and means "coal town." Easton (English, meaning "east-facing town") reached its best rank in 2015 at #78. Weston was #120 in 2015, also a best rank.

Dathan, Ethan, Jonathan, Jothan, Lathan, Nathan

Ethan (Hebrew, meaning "strength") is trending, hitting #2 in 2009 and 2010. Ethan was #6 in 2015. Jonathan is also Hebrew and means "gift of God." Jonathan has been in the top 50 since 1969 and was #48 in 2015. Nathan is from the same Hebrew root as Jonathan and means "gift." Nathan has been in the top 50 since 1975 and was #38 in 2015.

Alvin, Bevin, Braven, Calvin, Devin, Donovan, Draven, Elvin, Ervin, Evan, Gavin, Irvin, Ivan, Javon, Jovan, Kelvin, Kevin, Levin, Marvin, Mervin, Steven, Sullivan, Tavin, Trevon

Donovan is an Irish name meaning "dark brown," likely as a reference to someone with dark hair. Donovan came into the top 1000 in the U.S. in the 1900s and was #282 in 2015. Evan is a Welsh form of John, meaning "God is gracious." Evan has been in the top 100 in the U.S. since 1983 and was #67 in 2015. Ivan is the Russian form of John and is also popular in the U.S. Ivan was #138 in 2015. What about Tavin? Tavin is a form of Gustav, meaning "royal staff." 58 U.S. baby boys were named Tavin in 2015.

Bowen, Cohen, Darwin, Edwin, Elwin, Erwin, Ewan, Owen, Rowan, Sherwin

Ewan (pronounced Yoo-un) and Owen are both forms of the Gaelic name Eoghan, meaning "of the yew tree." There were 138 U.S. baby boys named Ewan in 2015. Owen is much more popular, at #36 in 2015. Rowan (Gaelic, meaning "little red-haired one") is a unisex name, currently more popular as a boy's name. In 2015, Rowan ranked #219 for U.S. baby boys and #331 for U.S. baby girls.

Banyan, Bryan, Canyon, Cian, Cleon, Deon, Finnian, Gideon, Ian, Kenyon, Kian, Leon, Lyon, Orion, Ryan, Zion

Have you considered Banyan, named for the tree in India? There were 24 U.S. baby boys name Banyan in 2015. What about Canyon? There were 114 U.S. baby boys named Canyon in 2015. Like many other Hebrew/Biblical names for boys, Gideon had its best year in 2015, at #328. Gideon means "mighty warrior." Orion (pronounced oh-RYE-on) is a name from Greek Mythology and a constellation. Orion came into the top 1000 in the '90s and was #368 in 2015. Keep in mind that some may mistake it for O'Ryan.

Boy names ending with a "p" or "r" sound

Bishop, Cap, Chip, Flip, Kip, Phillip, Pip, Shep, Skip, Tripp, Winthrop

Kip is short for Kipton or Kipling. There were 46 U.S. baby boys named Kip in 2015. Phillip is Greek and means "lover of horses." Phillip was #410 in 2015, quite a drop after being in the top 100 from 1937 to 1991. Philip (with one L) was #434. Tripp is a word name that sometimes refers to a third boy. Tripp came into the top 1000 in 2008 and was #686 in 2015.

Bear, Heber, Timber, Wilbur

There were 134 U.S. baby boys named Bear in 2015. If you like Bear, you might like Timber. There were 40 boys and 83 girls named Timber in 2015.

Archer, Catcher, Fletcher, Hatcher, Thatcher

Archer, an English occupational name, dropped out of the top 1000 in 1889 and made a comeback in 2009. Archer was #289 in 2015. Fletcher was #666 in 2015. Thatcher reached the top 1000 for the first time ever in 2013 and was #902 in 2015.

Alexander, Calder, Cedar, Evander, Fielder, Lander, Leander, Lysander, Olivander, Ryder, Salvador, Theodore, Vander, Wilder, Zander

Alexander, a Greek name that means "defender of mankind," was #8 in 2015. Alexander has been in the top 50 in the U.S. since 1985. Ryder is an English surname that means "horseman" or "knight." Ryder came into the top 1000 in 1994 and just reached top 100. Ryder was #98 in 2015. Wilder is a German surname that just reached the top 1000 in 2015 at #964.

Christopher, Kiefer, Topher

Christopher (Greek, "bearer of Christ") has been in the top 100 since 1949 and was #32 in 2015. There were 5 U.S. baby boys named Topher in 2015. Kiefer is a German surname that means "barrel maker." Kiefer had a short stint in the top 1000 from 1990-1991. In 2015 there were 26 baby boys named Kiefer and 6 named Keifer.

Edgar, Greer, Gregor, Jagger

Edgar, an Old English name meaning "wealthy spear," was #317 in 2015. Jagger is an English occupational surname that means "peddler" and of course also linked with the Rolling Stones. Jagger came into the top 1000 U.S. baby names in 2001 and was #657 in 2015.

Briar, Lior, Pierre

Briar is a unisex name that means "thorny bush," and has the distinction of reaching the top 1000 for both boys and girls for the first time in 2015. Briar was #998 for boys and #844 for girls. Lior, pronounced LEE-or is a Hebrew name meaning "my light." There were 26 boys and 7 girls given the name Lior in 2015.

Bridger, Granger, Major, Ranger, Roger

Bridger is an Old English name that means "lives near the bridge." Bridger first came into the top 1000 in 1999 and left the list last year. There were 197 U.S. baby boys named Bridger in 2015. Major can refer to the military rank or its Latin meaning, "superior" or "greater." Major dropped out of the top 1000 in the 1970s, but came back in 2010 at #882 and was #360 in 2015.

Becker, Booker, Brecker, Decker, Iker, Oscar, Packer, Parker, Riker, Striker, Tucker, Walker

Becker and Packer are two German occupational surnames. Becker means "baker" and Packer means "wool packer." There were 26 U.S. baby boys name Becker and 7 named Packer in 2015. A much more popular choice would be Parker, an English occupational surname that means "gamekeeper" and was #72 in 2015.

Blair, Chandler, Keller, Kyler, Miller, Sinclair, Skyler, Taylor, Tyler, Valor

Chandler is an Old French name that means "candle maker." Chandler first appeared in the top 1000 U.S. baby names in 1969 and was #423 in 2015. There were also 248 U.S. baby girls named Chandler in 2015. Kyler is a Dutch name that means "bowman." Kyler was #287 in 2015. There were also 94 U.S. baby girls named Kyler in 2015. Taylor (an English occupational name) is unisex, currently favoring girls. In 2015 Taylor was ranked #462 for boys and #76 for girls.

Amir, Cadmar, Delmar, Elmer, Homer, Jamar, Jamir, Kramer, Lamar, Mortimer, Namir, Omar, Palmer, Samir, Seymour

Amir is an Arabic name meaning "prince" or "commander." Amir was #188 in 2015 and has been in the top 1000 U.S. baby boy names since 1976. Jamir is a combination of Amir and Jamal created in the U.S. The combined meaning is "handsome prince." Jamir has been in the top 1000 since 2000 and was #695 in 2015. Samir is also Arabic and means "a companion to talk with at night." Samir came into the top 1000 in the 1970s just like Amir, but is not nearly as popular. Samir was #734 in 2015.

Abner, Banner, Brenner, Connor, Falkner, Garner, Gunner, Junior, Kenner, Sumner, Tanner, Turner, Wagner, Warner

Connor is an Irish name that means "hound lover." The Irish spelling is Conor. Connor was #54 in 2015. Conor was #477, Conner was #256, and Konnor was #851. Gunner has two possible origins. It may come from the Old English word "gonne or gunne" which referred to the person who loaded the weapons. Or as Gunnar, it's the Scandinavian version of Gunthar, meaning "bold warrior." Gunner was #238 in 2015. Gunnar was #386. Tanner is an English occupational surname that came into the top 1000 U.S. baby boy names in 1976. Tanner was #224 in 2015.

Caspar, Casper, Cooper, Draper, Gaspar, Hooper, Jasper, Roper, Trapper

Cooper is an English occupational name for a barrel or cask maker and was #77 in 2015. Casper, Gaspar and Jasper are all variations of the name of the Magi and mean "treasure bearer." Jasper is by far the most popular in the U.S. (with some help from Stephenie Meyer's Twilight) and was #215 in 2015. 29 U.S. baby boys were named Gaspar and 86 were named Casper in 2015.

Asher, Fisher, Frasier, Lancer, Nasir, Spencer, Windsor

Asher is a Hebrew name that means "happy, blessed." Asher had its best rank ever in 2015 at #83. There were also 74 baby girls named Asher in 2015. Spencer is English and means "steward." Spencer was #252 in 2015. There were also 237 girls named Spencer in 2015.

Alastair, Carter, Colter, Cutter, Dexter, Dieter, Foster, Gunter, Hector, Hunter, Peter, Porter, Richter, Salvatore, Slater, Sylvester, Victor, Walter, Webster

Carter had its best rank ever in 2015 at #24. Carter is an English occupational surname for someone who transports items by cart. Karter was #183. Hector is a Greek name that means "holding fast." Hector was #303 in 2015. Hunter, meaning "to hunt," was #41 in 2015. Porter has French and Latin origins and means either the occupation or "gatekeeper." Porter was #375 in 2015. Slater is an English occupational surname for a slate maker. There were 49 baby boys named Slater in 2015.

Arthur, Gunther, Luther, Macarthur

Arthur is a Celtic name that means "bear." Arthur was a top 20 name from 1880 to 1926 and was #292 in 2015. Luther is German and means "soldier of the people." Luther was often given to boys to honor Martin Luther, the reformer, and later Martin Luther King, the civil rights leader. Luther dropped out of the top 1000 in 1994. There were 99 U.S. baby boys named Luther in 2015.

Denver, Grover, Gulliver, Iver, Javier, Oliver, River, Silver, Trevor, Xavier

Denver is a place name, and from its French origins means "from Anvers." Denver dropped out of the top 1000 U.S. baby boy names in 2001, and just made it back in 2015 at #900. There were also 197 baby girls named Denver. Javier (pronounced hah-vee-air) is a Spanish form of Xavier (pronounced EX-ay-vee-er or zay-vee-er). Xavier means "new house" from its Basque origins and "bright" in Arabic. Javier was #226 and Xavier was #90 in 2015.

Mayer, Sawyer, Sayer, Thayer

Sawyer is an English occupational surname for someone who cuts wood. Sawyer came into the top 1000 for U.S. baby boys in 1991 and was #94 in 2015, its best rank ever (Sawyer reached the top 1000 for U.S. baby girls in 2010 and was #260 in 2015). Thayer is the French form of Taylor, the English occupational surname. There were 51 U.S. baby boys named Thayer in 2015.

Cesar, Ebenezer

Cesar is the Spanish form of Caesar, meaning "head of hair," and also an imperial title used during the Roman Empire. Cesar was #280 in 2015. There were also 91 baby boys with the original spelling, Caesar. Ebenezer is a Hebrew name meaning "stone of help," but probably better linked with Ebenezer Scrooge. There were 49 U.S. baby boys name Ebenezer in 2015.

Boy names ending with an "s" or "sh" sound (single syllable names first)

Ace, Boyce, Brice, Brooks, Bruce, Case, Chance, Chase, Chris, Claus, Dice, Gus Hans, Ives, Jace, Jens, Jess, Joss, Kierce, Lance, Lars, Mace, Pace, Parks, Phelps, Piers, Pierce, Price, Quince, Rance, Rhys, Rice, Ross, Royce, Russ, Spence, Trace, Tyce, Vance, Vince, Wes, Yates

Ace (Latin, meaning "one") was #418 in 2015. Chase is from Old French and means "to hunt." Chase was #74 in 2015. Rhys is a Welsh name meaning "ardor." The American spelling, Reese, is being taken over by baby girls (#173 for girls in 2015 vs #701 for boys). Rhys was #513 for boys in 2015. Ross is a Scottish name that means "headland." There were 157 U.S. baby boys named Ross in 2015.

Albus, Amos, Anders, Andres, Angus, Atlas, Atticus, Augustus, Aurelius, Caius, Carlos, Cassius, Christos, Clarence, Claudius, Clemens, Columbus, Curtis, Cyrus, Dallas, Darius, Davis, Demarcus, Demetrius, Dennis, Douglas, Elias, Ellis, Ennis, Enos, Erasmus, Erastus, Fergus, Ferris, Gervais, Harris, Hollis, Horace, Jarvis, Jesus, Jonas, Julius, Laurence, Lazarus, Linus, Lewis, Lucas, Lucius, Luis, Magnus, Marcellus, Marcos, Marcus, Mathis, Maurice, Maximus, Memphis, Midas, Milos, Mingus, Morris, Moses, Nicolas, Norris, Otis, Paris, Petros, Phineas, Rasmus, Remus, Reynolds, Sanders, Santos, Seamus, Septimus, Severus, Silas, Sirius, Stavros, Terrence, Thaddeus, Thomas, Titus, Tobias, Torrance, Travis, Tyrese, Ulysses, Wallace, Willis, Zaccheus, Zacharias, Zenos

Atticus is a newly trending name, coming into the top 1000 in 2004 and reaching #350 in 2015. Atticus is Latin and means "from Attica." Cyrus is a Persian name that means "throne." Cyrus was #472 in 2015. Ferris is an Irish name that means "rock." Ferris hasn't been in the top 1000 since 1922, and it may be far enough away from that mischievous Ferris Bueller for a comeback. There were 44 baby boys named Ferris in the U.S. in 2015. Seamus (pronounced SHAY-mus) is an Irish form of James, meaning "supplanter." Seamus reached the top 1000 U.S. baby boy names in 1995 and was #948 in 2015.

Ash, Cash, Dash, Dinesh, Hirsh, Nash, Marsh, Parish, Rush, Walsh

Cash, an Irish surname, was in the top 1000 a few times in the 1880s and 1890s, but made a comeback in 2003, the year Johnny Cash died. Cash was #267 in 2015 (Kash was 382). Nash is an English surname that means "at the ash tree." Nash was #344 in 2015.

Boy names ending with a "t" or "th" sound

Abbott, August, Albert, Art, Barnett, Barrett, Beckett, Benedict, Bennett, Bert, Brandt, Brent, Brett, Bryant, Cabot, Chet, Clement, Clint, Colt, Corbett, Cort, Crist, Curt, Darett, Delmont, Dwight, Earnest, Elliot, Emmett, Ernst, Everest, Everett, Flint, Forrest, Frost, Garrett, Gilbert, Grant, Hamlet, Hart, Harvest, Helmut, Herbert, Hewett, Holt, Hoyt, Hyatt, Jarrett, Jett, Kent, Lafayette, Lamont, Matt, Nate, Pete, Pilot, Rhett, Robert, Rupert, Sargent, Scott, Sennett, Slate, Stewart, Taggart, Talbot, Tate, Trent, Truitt, Vincent, West, Whit, Wright, Wyatt

Beckett reached the top 1000 U.S. baby boy names in 2006 and was #218 in 2015. Beckett is English and means "beehive." Bennett, a form of Benedict, meaning "blessed," has been in the top 1000 since the SSA started charting, but reached a new best in 2015 at #153. Emmett has also jumped recently, thanks to the –ett trend for boy names and Stephenie Meyer's Twilight. Emmett is actually a form of Emma, meaning "universal." However, there were only 13 baby girls named Emmett in 2015. Emmett was #139 for U.S. baby boys. Wyatt, an English name that means "strong in war," is also very popular right now, reaching #34 in 2015.

Braith, Ellsworth, Gareth, Garth, Griffith, Heath, Keith, Kenneth, Laith, Leith, North, Perth, Seth, Wentworth

Griffith is a Welsh name that means "strong lord." Griffith was in the top 1000 U.S. baby boy names only once, in 1899. There were 13 U.S. baby boys named Griffith in 2015. Keith is Scottish and means "woodland." Keith was a top 50 name from 1952-1978 and was #425 in 2015. Seth was in the top 100 for most of the 1980s and 1990s, but is one of the few Hebrew/Biblical names on a downward trend. Seth, meaning "appointed," was #278 in 2015.

Boy names ending with a "v" or "x" sound

Aviv, Cleve, Clive, Dave, Dev, Dov, Gustave, Lev, Reeve, Steve, Tove, Zev

Dev can be short for the Indian name Deval, meaning "divine" or the Irish name Devin, meaning "poet" or "fawn." In 2015 there were 105 baby boys named Dev. Reeve is from Middle English and means "bailiff." There were 37 U.S. baby boys named Reeve in 2015.

Alex, Bronx, Calix, Dax, Derex, Dex, Fairfax, Felix, Fox, Halifax, Hendrix, Jarvix, Jax, Jex, Knox, Lennox, Lex, Maddox, Max, Pax, Phoenix, Rex, Terex, Tex

There were 110 U.S. baby boys named Bronx in 2015. The Bronx in New York was originally named after Jonas Bronck. There were 193 baby boys named Fox in 2015. I like Phoenix, the Greek name that means "dark red" and the name of the mythical bird that symbolizes immortality. Phoenix reached the top 1000 for U.S. baby boys in 1995 and was #307 in 2015.

Boy names ending with a "z" sound

Blaze, Boaz, Charles, Cortez, Cruz, Dez, Forbes, Franz, Fritz, Hans, Hayes, Ives, James, Laz, Marquez, Miles, Niles, Ramses, Reeves, Rhodes

Cortez is a Spanish name that means "courteous." Cortez came into the top 1000 in the 1970s and dropped off in 2013. There were 191 U.S. baby boys named Cortez in 2015. Cruz is also Spanish and means "cross." Cruz was #324 in 2015. There were also 27 U.S. baby girls named Cruz in 2015. Hayes is an older name that came back into the top 1000 in 2009 and continues to rise. Hayes, an English name that means "hedged land," was #539 in 2015.